The Nine Powers of Women

Awakening the Divine Feminine Within

BY ANA BARRETO

BOOKS BY ANA BARRETO

Women, Rice and Beans: Nine Wisdoms I Learned from My Mother When I Really Paid Attention

Self-Trust: A Healing Practice for Women Who Do Too Much

There is a Higher Power Within: 28 Meditation Prompts to Find Peace & Happiness Within

PROGRAMS BY ANA BARRETO

Finding a Greater Wellbeing in a Busy World: Meditation

Making Space for a Loving Relationship

Discover Your Purpose & Mission

Nine Powers of Women Quantum Activation Program – Healing Through the Chakras

HOW TO CONNECT ONLINE:

Visit http://www.ana-barreto.com for meditations, classes, and inspirational content

Like my page on Facebook: @ana1barreto

Follow me on Instagram: @ana1barreto

Follow me on Twitter: @ana1barreto

Follow me on Pinterest: @ana1barreto

Send your comments, questions, and concerns to ana@ana-barreto.com

1st Edition, January 2022

ISBN-978-0-9979006-9-9

Blue Hudson Group, Albany, NY

I dedicate this book to my grandmother Maria,
my mother Aracy,
my daughters Erica and Isabel,
my stepdaughters Cindy, Janet, and Christine,
my nieces Andrea, Beatriz, Luiza, and Leticia,
and to all women who will read these words and awaken
their Divine Feminine within.

Contents

The Divine Pearl

*A new season of women's lives is about to awaken. There is
a calling in the air to be answered with the heart. It smells like
a new beginning; It tastes like courage and feels like a belated
bloom. Today, you have arrived in your own Spring.*

I have wanted to change the world since I was nine years old,
but I was told I couldn't even take out the garbage because I was
a girl. It was a mundane task that had considerable implications
on the existence and roles of women.

Today, getting my children to take out the garbage is like asking
them to give up their kidneys. But when I was a child in Brazil, it
was an act of freedom as a woman. The few times I did it, I had to
hide it from my father. He was steadfast in his belief that boys did
outside work and girls helped inside the house.

As I grew up, I soon discovered that what seemed to be a single
incident of gender discrimination was actually a global pandemic
of its own. Women's ways were misunderstood and marginalized
for centuries (and still are to a large degree). Time made this marginalization "acceptable," religion justified it, and justice looked
the other way in order to avoid disrupting what had always been.

Yet when I moved to New York, I saw that the educated women
in the Empire State were much more advanced in voicing their
freedom and becoming who they wanted to be compared to the

women in Brazil in the late eighties. American women were asking the questions that helped them take their proper place in history.

One of the things I have learned over the years is that women think differently than men. We know this because science has found it to be true, not to mention the fact that men so often look at us as though we have two heads.

What happens to one woman happens to all women. You may not have experienced violence yourself, but you can feel it through the stories of other women shared with their own breath. This violence and marginalization have happened even though women have special powers. That's right: *you have powers*. They aren't the type of superpowers you read in comic books or see in Hollywood movies. Your powers are real powers, and when used appropriately, they can help you build a good life. These powers are not for fighting against men, systems, religions, or laws. Their purpose is to support the world and improve the quality of life for everyone.

It feels like I stumbled on the Nine Powers of Women by accident, but there are no accidents in life. We create the so-called "accidents" we experience. The inability to simply take out the trash because of my gender wasn't an accident. It was a catalyst that drove me to question, search, and study my lack of power and then develop my specific feminine powers.

Your powers are your natural ways of being a woman. They may have been called a distraction, a weakness, or even witchcraft. But once you remember, understand, and feel them in their natural strength, they will change everything for you. And you'll no longer have to justify how you nurture yourself, solve problems, communicate, work with others, or take higher leadership roles. You'll be able to do all of those things and more without changing who you are.

You are the pearl of the world. All of the grains of pain our ancestors endured that are described in women's history are now the precious treasure we unveil to redefine our place in history. Know your worth. You are one of a kind. You are divine.

An Open Letter to Women from the Ancients

My Dear Woman,

We love you.

We love you as a sister, as a mother, and as a daughter.

We are connected in heart.

Together, we are one, even though we don't come from the same family, background, or country. We may not believe in the same religion, government, or science. We may not recognize the same God. We may not follow the same role models or speak the same language. We certainly have different skin colors, hair, and fashion styles. Our eyes look at a different ground but see the same stars. We hear different sounds, but when we touch others, our intentions align.

Despite all of this, our Divine Feminine spirit has transcended time and space, writing the stories we all live, breathe, and sometimes forget. In that way, we are also connected at a soul level.

You arrived at this book through an invitation that was written thousands and thousands of years before you were born. Eve had an intention, which you will learn more about as you keep reading. We knew you would come to discover your truth. Welcome. Be calm. You have a special place at this table.

As you read these words, we ask that you read them with your heart. Your brain is likely to deny much of it and try to toss it out. Yet your heart will contemplate the wisdom that already exists inside you. Be certain that your heart will remember what your mind will want to forget.

If the reading bothers you at your core, we ask you that you read it again and again. Our intent is to disrupt most of what has been written about women and awaken your infinite feminine power. It's for your benefit that you consider the alternatives and question every bit of wisdom as you discover the insights yourself. We don't have all the pieces; no one does. These words are simply a good starting point to remove you from the status quo.

Unfortunately, the history of female wisdom lost its foundation in the books written by men. Some of the knowledge has been mistranslated, misinterpreted, and burned in a fire. Some women were forced into forgetfulness by fear. Some have survived by the pure determination of the Divine Feminine that lives inside us and is waiting to be individually awakened.

Your individual goals and desires contribute to the evolution of women, society, and the planet. Regardless of your intentions, which may be self-centered or philanthropic, career or family-oriented, local or global in scale, all outcomes will take us forward. The success or shortcoming of your personal mission will still impact the feminine consciousness that is continuously evolving, but this time, the evolution will be faster. Our old strategy – patience – is becoming obsolete. Although patience is still in use, it is only a brief state to hear the wisdom available to you. The new strategy is to Take Small Actions. You are called to use as many powers as you can and as often as you are willing and able to.

Some of the insights you experience will make you angry. Some will make you cry, and most of it will make you think, feel, and go beyond where you were before. Our goal is to propel your life forward and improve the overall quality of your life. This is our gift to you.

We are gifting this book to you, not because you might need it, but because we all do. By giving it to you, we are reminded of our commitment to the women we are becoming or unbecoming, as well as our vow to awaken our Divine Feminine and live up to our highest potential.

We have witnessed that the more you care for yourself, the more other women will care for themselves. The more other women care for themselves, the more our daughters and granddaughters will make it a way of life. We are praying for a cycle of caring, well-being, and evolution of women so large that everyone can touch, feel, taste, and own it in their innermost sacred being. The day you were born, you carried the vow to restore the existence of all women who lived before you.

Be happy. Be courageous. Be authentic.
The world is waiting for you.

Sincerely,
The Women of the Ancients

The Story of Women

This is one of the stories I've learned about women. It was put together with many sources but not proven. Some believe it's a myth, but myths often contain some truth.

In her book, *The Goddess and God of Old Age*, archeologist Marija Gimbutas argues that women were priestesses and held prominent positions in the government in ancient times. At the same time, the men did physical chores such as hunting and building. She says that the ancient people worshiped goddesses and lived in peace because those deities represented female traits. In her theory, Gimbutas shares that these peaceful societies were destroyed by Indo-Europeans, the vanguard of today's Western civilization responsible for the world's economic, environmental, and political crises. Not surprisingly, Gimbutas was discredited by her male contemporaries. But let's explore this theory.

Long ago, the earth was created. It was a beautiful planet. It was decided that it would be a center for all worlds even though the earth was only one of many inhabited planets. Many regions on earth were populated, and women ruled them because of their wisdom. They didn't govern with the mind but with the heart and the power of their feelings.

Other worlds envied earth and wanted it for their own enjoyment. They knew how powerful women leaders were and began to kill the heads of government. As a result, women became infected with a disease: *fear*.

As word spread that female leaders were dying, envious men saw an opportunity to take over and convinced the rest of the women to hide and relinquish their powers along with their right to lead. Many women were killed, and the men began to rule. The "fear disease" changed women's awareness, and their powers were forgotten for generation after generation.

Over the centuries, some women could feel their powers returning. Unfortunately, those brave women were quickly marginalized, imprisoned, or put to death. Remember the witches killed in history? Many of them had awakened their energy or were sympathizers of the women with power.

This story cannot be proven, but many people have shared it. The same way science has discovered the hidden powers of prayer, meditation, heart energy, brain capabilities, the mind of the heart, past lives, energy fields, and other unexplained subjects of the past, it will only be a matter of time before the history of women can be entirely known and accepted.

Why Do Women Need to Awaken Their Powers?

Time and time again, women have existed in obscurity, convinced that we're not good enough to do anything except bear male children and manage the house. Even birthing a daughter is a reason to mourn, and many mothers and daughters have lost their lives because of it.

Of course, we have evolved considerably since those times. We have shown our capabilities, but we often have to work twice as hard, give up our personal goals, and justify our family life to have our ambitions fed. Women with potential often have to fit into the narrow mold created by the few men in charge, and there are usually no women in the group that makes decisions that impact women.

Women are still frequently overlooked today based on their marital status, color, weight, background, motherhood decisions, and sexuality. Then, if they meet the "criteria," they're often overlooked because of how women think, how much they talk, and how they lead even if they get great results. It's time to change all of this.

The main reason for women to awaken our power is to save the planet. The beautiful earth needs yin energy, the female power, to become balanced. Currently, the world is too yang. Women's energy and the decisions that will come from us will preserve the planet's beauty and create equilibrium.

We don't need to take control of the world; we only need to balance the energy in the pockets of the world we live in. It may seem a vast and daunting job, but it isn't. I believe that we need to return to our natural ways of being, exercise our rights, and take small actions in our lives to do what we feel called to do. I know that time is on our side. We have not gotten here overnight, and we have an eternity to get where we need to be. Our daughters and granddaughters will take over what we start.

The Energy of Cooperation

There are groups of people who believe women will never work together. It seems they are counting on women to act jealously and have quarrels. They justify this thinking based on the misconception that when women live together in the same household, they synchronize their periods, which they believe is meant to eliminate competition among them. This misogynistic thought sees competition as a way to win and filters behaviors through the lenses of rivalry, competition, opposition, and war.

It isn't a competitive strategy when one woman isn't available for sex with men, and the sisters immediately become unavailable. It is about collaboration, compassion, and harmony. The reason women tend to mimic each other's cycles is because of our innate ways of sharing compassion for one another. There is comfort in sharing experiences between a circle of women. In the past, they looked forward to those days when womanhood was celebrated. Any discomfort felt by one was lessened by the sisterhood around them. Nature ensured collaboration became a means of survival.

The body always seeks harmony. Natural synchronization is a process we see everywhere.

Sure, women have exhibited envy, but it's a learned behavior from those who seek to thrive in competition. Naturally, right-brained people, primarily women, interpret competitive behaviors as jealousy. I'm not saying that jealous women don't exist, only that this is not a natural state for them. We mimic the people around us in their pursuit of success. Unfortunately, they compete for limited resources, not realizing that resources are limitless.

People who see the glass as half empty instead of half full and believe that most people are competitive will filter every scenario through those lenses. What they fail to understand is that survival is actually the result of cooperation.

In 1866, the theory of "Survival of the Fittest" was developed by Charles Darwin and Alfred Wallace as the process of natural selection, which states that survival odds are higher for those who can adapt. This concept is often taught in schools and continues to reinforce the myth that competition is necessary. Yet, new studies have debunked the idea that competition is vital for survival, and many even say that this wasn't Darwin's intention. Actually, when you look at history, cooperation is the key to flourishing cultures.

It isn't too late for today's women to fully benefit from activating and owning our power and letting go of the idea of a competitive world. As we awaken these powers, we will acquire more self-knowledge, increased self-care, creativity, confidence, authenticity, and intuition. Our actions today will organically benefit future generations. Girls aged one to nine will develop these powers in their subconscious minds even if we don't pull them into a classroom and teach them. They will learn by osmosis because as more women demonstrate their feminine powers, it will be contagious.

Living in the core of our feminine power is the key to our progress as women. We must start now so that our daughters, granddaughters, and great-granddaughters have more opportunities to experience womanhood free of stigmas and criticisms about their rights, desires, and ambitions. They will have the chance to use their gifts and exercise their natural powers for the world's welfare. When a woman is well, everyone around her is well.

Adam Was Probably a Jerk

We learn from stories. The tribal mind told stories to share the past, learn from it, and curb the behavior of the tribe members. People use stories to preserve their culture and honor their ancestors' history. These days, scholars call it mythology and accept the stories as folklore.

When we hear about humanity's beginnings, for example, we learn the story of Adam, Eve, and the beautiful Garden of Eden. In this paradise, people were meant to live happily ever after until Eve supposedly screwed it up for everyone. The Bible made it real, and today, thousands of years later, people still blame Eve and link her to the devil. But what if that story was made up? What if the story was embellished as we do when we retell stories and add our own bits to them? What if Adam, Eve, and paradise were folklore?

I would like you to consider this version of the story. I'm not ditching the Bible, but I'm considering an alternative since some aspects of this old tale have been confirmed and others dismissed by science as a result of new discoveries. In addition, many of the ancient scrolls used to create the Bible are now being corrected since they found many discrepancies in the translations, and we also have a better understanding of human nature today.

We are told that God created Adam, and then God created Eve from Adam's rib. Adam and Eve lived in the Garden of Eden happily. A few scholars have located the actual place of the garden with some agreement between them. It's believed that it was in

Sumer, the birthplace of humanity. Although it's a dry desert today, in those times, it was lush and green.

In 1684, Pope Clement XI and his bishops revised the Bible. They removed fourteen books from the original version and changed some translations into what we read today. The story of Adam and Eve and the Garden of Eden stayed.

In 1922, old Sumerian tablets were found in a cave dated 4500 BC and translated. French author and researcher of ancient civilizations Anton Parks, who studied the old Sumerian texts, found many discrepancies in the translations. He reported that some of the text was mistranslated, and essential parts were omitted. The archeologists who translated those texts in 1922 were funded by Biblical societies attempting to prove the Bible as a historical fact. Thus, they may have had an incentive to report what their funders wanted to hear.

One of the mistranslations found by Parks was that the Garden of Eden was a place for animals, not a paradise. Also, there are mentions of many gods and even a god with reptile features that created humans to release the gods from their daily heavy work. The tablets read that the gods created humans from their DNA to serve the gods. The humans were slaves and lived lives of suffering. These gods called the humans "animals." Anton also discovered the origin of the word "Adam," which means "animal."

So, the story of Adam and Eve, as told in the Bible texts we read today, doesn't hold up. According to the story we've all been told, they were the only humans on earth, but the old texts say otherwise. Why would God only create one man and one woman? Did their children have incestuous relationships in order to populate the world? How about the Tree of Knowledge? Why would God forbid humans from knowing? If the Garden of Eden was paradise on earth, why move it to heaven, the place we wait to reach when we die? Do these ideas seem like an act of God to you or of humans?

What if the story was written or adapted by people who wanted to influence humans to behave in a certain way? Why would they go to such lengths to discredit, shame, and disarm women? What influence did women have that threatened men or their ways of organizing?

When I think about these questions, I see a different scenario. I believe that the paradise described as the Garden of Eden was a slave farm managed by powerful beings that people called gods. The ancient scrolls tell us that there were two gods called Enlil and Enki, who had opposing agendas. Enlil believed humans were inferior beings and were created to serve the gods. Enki knew that humans had in their DNA the ability to be like gods and should be allowed to flourish and be free.

In 1987 scientists discovered a well-preserved fossil of an infant carbon-dated thirty thousand years old. They were able to extract DNA from the bones, and the results indicated that today's humans appeared all of a sudden about three thousand years ago and that we aren't, as previously believed, descendants or close relatives of Neanderthals.

I also believe that there were other humans on earth and on the farm. Why have only two slaves when you can have hundreds? The men went out to hunt, and the women farmed and raised animals in paradise.

Enki had reptile features, but in the modern translations, he was depicted as a serpent that tricked Eve into eating the forbidden apple. I suspect that Enki visited the humans often and that he was fascinated by them. He approached the women because they were around all day farming while the men were hunting. Also, he must have seen their potential. Eve or any other woman on the slave farm would have access to this "god" who wanted to help the humans. It's possible that Enki talked with Eve and taught her about the powers of humans, and she was clever enough to learn, practice, and teach those powers to others, including Adam and other women.

We read in the Bible that God is within, and so are His power: "God is love, and whoever abides in love abides in God, and God abides in him." (John 4:16)

There is also an account of a battle where the humans revolted against the gods, and many died. The few left were returned to slavery, but there is no mention of it in the current Bible.

It's very unlikely that Adam and Eve were kicked out of the slave farm by the gods. They must have survived because we hear of their offspring, so they probably fled the area.

I believe that there are two possibilities of why Eve's reputation and the reputation of women in history got destroyed, one that started with the bad god Enlil and another with Adam. The god Enlil must have felt threatened that his slaves would begin to think for themselves or use their intuition as Eve did, so he did whatever possible to not lose control of them. He discouraged the slaves by sharing stories of what Eve's and Adam's lives were like outside the Garden of Eden, which we still hear of today. Also, through the text, we learn that the god Enki later left the area. He was considered to be the devil.

The second possibility of women's inherited poor reputation may have started with Adam. With a dominant left-brain that thrives in organizations and systems, Adam probably struggled to live outside the slave camp of Eden. There, he knew where to hunt, what to eat, and where to sleep. You can imagine how furious Adam was at Eve for having initiated the change. I suspect that he blamed her for the rest of their lives for leaving his paradise. Adam might have told and retold the story to their children, grandchildren, and neighbors, who then told other people. He might even have shamed Eve every time things didn't happen his way. Unfortunately, Eve's courageous action escaping the slave camp never got into the history books because the truth wouldn't help curb women's behavior.

Like many other women who avoid conflict, Eve stayed quiet and hoped that others would see that humans have benefited from the change. She hoped they would recognize the benefits of living outside slavery. But many cultures assimilated the story and made sure women would have no powers to make decisions. Religion embellished the story for its own gain in order to control people and decided that the pain of childbirth was a punishment God inflicted upon women due to Eve's actions.

But let's be realistic here. Men are considered the brains of math, mechanics, and physics. But they can't figure out that the pain of childbirth is simple science? Try to squeeze an average baby head, which is thirteen inches in circumference and four and a half inches in diameter, through a vagina that ranges from two-point-one to four-point-seven-five inches. That's going to hurt.

So why would the gods fear women? What threatening powers do women possess? Why do male religious, governmental, and business leaders so often feel intimidated by the participation of women? Why would they discredit women and connect them with the devil when the concept of Satan didn't exist until much later? By the way, the word "Satan" means to hold a grudge and cherish animosity.

Even the story of Lucifer, the angel who disobeyed God by bringing fire to humans, is questionable. Knowing what we know today about the comfort of a fire, why wouldn't God want us to have it?

Let's assume for one moment that the Bible story of Eve is true. If the word "Satan" means to hold a grudge, who is it who's holding the grudge?

The Creator, the Infinite Love, Powerful and Merciful God does not hold grudges – men do.

Unless scientists can find a way to create human beings in a laboratory, the future of humanity depends on women. Until then, women are creators. Would God, the master creator, bestow his best work of art to an inferior being? I don't see humans being born out of butterflies or trees. If women are creators, why would God create the man first and then take one of his ribs to create one woman? This seems like a man's fairytale. Women bring vast contributions to humanity, and unfortunately, too many people are afraid of their capabilities.

How Powerful Are You?

"The most common way people give up their power
is by thinking they don't have any."

— ALICE WALKER

I walked into this book barefooted and dressed in moral courage. With the help of God, I surrendered and became unattached to any results. I carry only one raw intention: to break the spells humanity has cast on women. This partnership with the spirit and our female ancestors has the intent not to fight anyone or existing systems but to invite these life-breathers to awaken their powers and use their talents to bring an equilibrium to the world our children will inherit. Fighting anything will only solidify the status quo.

This is also a call from Mother Nature. She is inviting more women to step into their power and expand the yin energy to balance the yang energy we experience today.

You're called to be the light to balance the darkness, the water to flow with fire, and the moon to support the sun. But again, fighting will perpetuate the misunderstanding of the brilliance women bring to the table.

Women have an enormous amount of power. The Mother made sure of it. However, when we witness the masculine energy over-powering our systems, we wouldn't know it. So we need to dig deeper.

When you look at the representation of the universe, you find the symbol of yin and yang divided into two areas: matter and spirit. Yin – earth; yang – heaven. They aren't in opposition to each other; they complement one another. Yin and yang represent the balance of male-female energy. The male is characterized by the white area of the image and the female by the dark area. You can also see that the yin area has a dot of the yang, and the yang area has a dot of the yin. This reminds us that both energies, which seem to be opposing forces, are actually complementary.

It's all about harmony. Yang cannot exist without yin.

YIN	YANG
Earth	Heaven
Inner	Outer
North	South
Negative	Positive
Female, Soft	Male, Hard
Dark, Night	Light, Day
Cold	Hot
Passive	Active
Receptive	Creative

We learn from nature that there's a constructive expression of power. If yang is too dominant, yin will grow. It has to, or yang will diminish. And because yang energy is overgrown already, yin energy needs expansion now.

Both powers need each other to exist—the cold needs the hot, and the negative needs the positive. Think of yin-yang energy in terms of a cup of tea. The cup is an outer shell—solid, hard, and yang. The cup alone has no use to anyone until we see the empty space inside, which is the yin, the tea.

Unfortunately, because of its passive nature, yin energy is often overlooked. Yin is receptive, inner-directed, and quiet. It attracts. In contrast, yang is active, outer-directed, and competitive. It repels, and its nature calls for notoriety.

To further understand this yin-yang dance, think of the words on this page. See yang as the words and yin as the spaces in between. Without the spaces between the words, a bunch of letters would be pushed together so that you couldn't discern the meaning they're trying to convey.

Although yin is retractive, it has tremendous power. Look at the Grand Canyon formation. The solid, majestic, hard rock's yang formation was shaped by water, which is soft, flowing yin energy.

Can you see the need for female encrgy and its true essence? The real question is: *can you feel humanity calling for you?* If you don't know and understand your power, you are giving it away. We need women to balance the planet's energy, and we can do that by stepping into the power that's unique to women.

When women are well, all people around them—children, men, and women—are well. And I don't mean that women will cook, clean, feed, and look after others like most of us do. Our feminine energy is more powerful than that. With intention alone, we can light up the world. This power is magnified when women are aligned in groups, even when they aren't in the same space but have the same intentions. Women can uplift the planet. This is not a small task, but we were born with the gift to do it.

It's a Crisis of Confidence

The history of women and the ways women were viewed and treated over centuries have led people to believe that women are powerless, but we are far from it. Many women have stopped thinking for themselves and speaking their minds over the centuries because that was expected of them. Many have pretended and more recently acted like a man to share their ideas or fulfill their mission, while others swallowed their talents and made a conscious decision to survive in the masculine world by playing small.

Because of the history we inherited, it isn't unusual for today's women to doubt their abilities and take a subtle approach toward archaic ideas that diminish women's natural ways of being and their contribution to the betterment of society.

In 2014, Goldman Sachs and Columbia University researchers determined that confidence is an important competency. A group of men and women with similar education and background were asked to take a test on their field of expertise. Then, before learning their results, they were asked to assess how they thought they did on the test. The majority of the women self-assessed themselves as having done worse than they actually did, while the men self-assessed themselves as having done better than they actually did. Later, the researcher asked them to take another test. This time, the men and women were asked to report the level of confidence in their answers. Again, the women's scores went down, while the men's improved. Even after telling women that they were better than they thought after the first test, women didn't improve their confidence levels while men did, knowing that their early self-assessment was inflated.

In a women's leadership development training that I created, high potential female managers were selected by their bosses to attend the training, which was designed to get them ready for promotion. More than half of the women self-assessed themselves as having medium or low confidence during the session. They didn't see themselves as high potential managers like their bosses did.

Another similar case happened with my client, Andrea. She was offered a promotion by her boss, but she turned it down. She felt she wasn't looking for a promotion at that time. Six months later, her boss's boss offered her an even better promotion. She was surprised by the offer and asked her immediate supervisor if he felt she was qualified to take the position. He snapped at her, "If I didn't think you were qualified for the job, my supervisor wouldn't have offered it to you."

What is the disconnect between women and their potential? Unfortunately, most women believe they are powerless and don't possess the capacity or potential they aspire. Are they delusional? Some people might say so, but I say that women have simply been misguided.

Every woman is born with powers that carry a level of energy in their bodies. These energy centers have unlimited potential when balanced and exercised. On the other hand, these centers can be out of balance or diminished when overused, ignored, or shot down by our choices and the environments we live in. The most common way women give their power away is by not knowing they have them.

Ancient Sanskrit described these energy centers centuries ago, first introduced in India between 1500 and 500 BC in the oldest text called the *Vedas*. They are also called chakras or wheels of life. Many people today have heard of the chakras of the body. Still, we don't associate them with improving our personal power and impacting the overall quality of our life.

What Are Your Powers and What Do They Do?

Women's powers are our gifts to mankind. I'm not being naïve or conceited when I say that, nor am I exaggerating. When women step into their power, they increase their level of consciousness. When they hear the wisdom of their energy and listen to it, their world improves, along with the people around them. Energetically, the world becomes a better place. Wouldn't you like to be part of it?

When I speak of power, I'm not talking about power *over* others. These are not powers to harvest and sell. We aren't talking about commodities to trade. They aren't the kinds of powers we see in *Wonder Woman* and *Superwoman*. They are real, true examples of empowerment that we have forgotten over the centuries.

Each of the Nine Powers is connected with one of the Seven Chakras of the body. We have Nine Powers and only Seven Chakras because three of the powers are linked to the Heart Center Chakra, which you will learn more about in the later chapters. There are three lower energy centers and four higher centers. Many spiritual teachers call the three lower chakras – the Root, Sacral, and Solar Plexus – the survival energy centers, but they are thriving chakras. Because many people have experienced most blockages in those three chakras, it doesn't mean that we treat them with prejudice. On the contrary, these three base chakras can be great foundations for the upper chakras, which are the altruistic and emotional chakras. They are the Heart, Throat, Third Eye, and Crown Centers.

As you learn about each power, you will also learn an overview of the Seven Chakras.

Here are the Nine Powers of Women:
1) Power of Nurturing
2) Power of Creativity
3) Power of Confidence
4) Power of Compassion
5) Power of Authenticity
6) Power of Intuition
7) Power of Beauty
8) Power of Generosity
9) Power of Healing

These powers fluctuate in intensity and expression throughout our lives. We received them when we were born, and during our childhood, unbeknownst to us, we grow, diminish, or hide them. Our parents, teachers, relatives, and friends are the catalysts for our decision to deal or not deal with our powers.

But don't worry, as our powers never cease to exist. They become dormant, but they can be reawakened. Some will be easily restored, while others might take some time. If you're willing to give yourself time, kindness, and forgiveness, you can revive all your powers.

These powers have an innate intelligence of their own. When one is depleted, it pulls energy from another to compensate for it. For example, when our Power of Compassion is blocked, we call on the Power of Creativity by drinking or doing drugs to manage the relationships that require our Power of Compassion. If our Power of Nurturing is weak, we use our Power of Intuition to protect ourselves by paying attention to the actions of others that might harm us, thus becoming more vigilant than we need to be. Although those temporary fixes work, those powers were not meant to be used that way – it's very inefficient.

Have you heard of a seventy-year-old grandmother who lifted a five-ton truck to rescue her grandson? Have you heard of the woman who canceled a trip only to discover that the plane she would have taken had crashed? How about the TV anchor who was fired for being too heavy, only to become the top TV anchor in America?

Thousands of women have been told they could never have children until they decided to adopt and later had their own biological children. The doctors can't explain the many cases of terminally ill people who cured themselves without any medical explanation other than calling it a miracle.

Until these experiences, all of these women were ordinary people. Then, they stepped into their power one day, and their lives changed forever. You can be one of them, too. There are no special pills or magic potions to transform your world and the world of the people around you. You only need your own powers. Don't be surprised as you read about each power that you remember them and feel more motivated about life. You had them all along. They just needed to be dusted off and cultivated.

These powers are essential for you to accomplish your mission and live purposefully. Once you own and exercise them, they will become a gift for others.

How to Read This Book

Each chapter contains information on one of the powers. In addition, individual chapters will give an in-depth review of their respective powers. You will learn what these powers do, why you need them, and how to use them. You'll be able to assess how much you have of each, how to awaken and develop them, what areas of your life you need to use them, and practical ways to activate them when you need them.

You can read the entire book and then return to the chapters you feel you need to work on the most, or you can go straight to a power you want to learn more about. The Further Resource chapter will give you additional guidance on what powers can help you with the issues you are currently experiencing. Feel free to dog-ear the pages, use a highlighter, and make notes in the margins. I suggest that you use a journal or purchase the book companion. You can also download a free PDF version of the book companion by visiting http://www.ana-barreto.com/ninepowers

Plan to access the *Nine Powers of Women Meditation* at any time for support. As you read each chapter, the meditation will help you align with your intention and open the pathways to master and use your powers. You will see that developing one of the nine will help you improve the other eight. The meditation is available for download at http://www.ana-barreto.com/ninepowers.

Another excellent resource for you is the Nine Powers of Women Quantum Activation Program – Healing Through the Chakras. This program will remove the unconscious barriers you carry about your powers and improve how you feel, think, and take action in your life. Based on the MAP System developed by Colette Streicher, this program is gentle, fast, and efficient by re-wiring your brain and helping you release any fears, traumas, and ideas that don't support the powerful woman you are becoming. You will receive the Nine Powers of Women Quantum Activation Program – Healing Through the Chakras #9 The Power of Healing with the book purchase. You can purchase individual programs for the powers you need, or the entire collection. Visit http://www.ana-barreto.com/ninepowers for more information

Try not to assume anything about the chapters before you read them. For example, some people may believe that chapter one—The Power of Nurturing—is about having children, but it isn't, although mothers certainly do use their nurturing powers. I don't want to give the chapter away, but let's just say that we are our second mothers. Do you get my drift?

Also, be gentle with yourself, and trust your intuition. This book is designed to disrupt your status quo and remind you that you may have been giving your power away. You will also find support for your new beliefs and winds of inspiration. I'm most excited about the level of courage you will discover so that you can take steps to live life on your own terms.

At a minimum, you will find peace of mind. Then, as you learn the wisdom of each power and receive insights about your long-time struggles, you'll let go of the ideas that contradict what your inner guidance knows about you. At this point, peace will arrive quietly and effortlessly in your life.

The world needs you as you truly are. Your unique female qualities bring a life force to a world that seeks equilibrium.

Thank you for playing your part, and enjoy the journey of transformation.

Chapter 1
The Power of Nurturing

*"Be there for others but never
leave yourself behind."*

— UNKNOWN

A woman wakes up in the morning and snoozes her clock twice until 6:15 a.m. But this day started yesterday at 8:00 p.m. when she got the children showered and had them select their clothes for the next day. She gets up feeling exhausted and grabs her phone to check for messages and emails. Before she drags herself to the shower, she wakes up the children by turning the lights on and nudging them gently. She gets dressed and checks on the children's morning progress. Do they have matching socks, and can they find the shoes? No one is allowed to change their minds about the clothes they selected last night.

She brushes their hair, nudging them for another decision: ponytail or pigtails. Most of the time, it will be a ponytail because the hair ties don't make it back to where they belong for pigtails. Then, she quickly moves them downstairs to the kitchen to eat a bowl of cereal with one percent organic milk. While the children eat their breakfast, she prepares their lunch and snacks for the day.

She knows she has to be inside the car by 7:25 a.m. at the latest, or she'll be behind the school bus or the garbage trucks on one-lane roads, which will make her late for work. The stress starts at 7:00 a.m. when she begins to rush the kids to stop talking, finish breakfast, and brush their teeth. The backpacks are left by the door with the lunch bags, and she calls for them again to get in the car.

She has a daily meeting at 8:30 a.m., and her boss closes the door at precisely 8:30 a.m., so latecomers can't go in. Before entering the car, she hugs the children and counts the hugs quickly. The older daughter had accused her of hugging her younger sister more often.

Most days, she leaves on time, drives to school, drops the children off, and rushes to work. Then, she parks the car and walks fast to the office to apply her makeup before the 8:30 a.m. meeting. She doesn't want to be the last person walking in the room, so she usually has ten minutes to accomplish that.

At the meeting, she reports the plans for the day and comments on yesterday's results. Many times, she doesn't have a chance to research it beforehand.

At 9:30 a.m., she gets a cup of coffee and a bagel to begin her office day, which is supposed to end at 6:00 p.m. She eats lunch late in her office and drinks another cup of coffee in the afternoon to get a second wind.

She cooks dinner on Sundays for the entire week to have more time during the week, so her goal is to be out of the office by 6:00 p.m. and have dinner with her children at 6:30 p.m. But at 5:55 p.m., the phone rings, and no one wants to answer because the late calls tend to last a while. She decides to answer the phone because the best business deals she's ever made have come from these late calls.

When she gets home, the children rush to her. They're so happy to see her and tell her everything about their day. And she lets them. They have dinner, and at 8:00 p.m., she gives them a bath, puts them in pajamas, and reads them a book. Then, she gives them a short back or foot rub and turns off the lights exactly at 8:30 p.m.

The next day, it all starts again, and she longs for the weekend when she hopes to take a nap.

* * *

That woman was me. At that time, I didn't know about the Power of Nurturing. When I discovered the first power that we develop in childhood, I was in my forties after having too many burnouts. I lived the rollercoaster of being well for a while and then burned out when I didn't listen to my body and pushed myself past my limits. Eventually, I found a way to heal the pattern with my inner powers.

The Power of Nurturing is also called *Mothering* or *Caring Power*. But calling it the Power of Nurturing helps encompass all of the qualities associated with this power. It makes it easy for women to identify, understand, and develop the energy that will keep them safe, secure, and nurtured.

In this chapter, I will also use the word *mother* often. The use of the word doesn't only imply the carrying of a baby in the womb or caring for a child. Today, many women have made the conscious decision to not have children. The Power of Nurturing is not only about motherhood but also about our ability to provide safety, security, and stability to ourselves first and then others—not necessarily just children.

The first Power of Women is located in the root chakra, which is the energy center area located at the bottom of the spine close to our sexual organs. It's energized by the color red and the earth element. Often called the earth chakra, this energy center is blocked by fear.

When we think of the "mother" and its most commonsense use of the word, mothering abilities are about nurturing, loving, caring for others, transmitting warm feelings of security, and creating a sense of stability with the help of the wisdom of our ancestors. We learn to be mothers from our mothers without proper instructions. The directions from many generations before are inscribed in our DNA.

As we travel to different cultures, we see the many deviations of the mother archetype we are most accustomed to. Some will depict a mother breastfeeding, while others will show a powerful woman at the head of the dinner table. Some will have the woman with a baby and a briefcase. Many will have the grandmothers watching over the children while the mother goes to work. Yet regardless of the mother archetype you subscribe to, the mothering power is innate, always available, and inextinguishable.

Changes in the Nurturing Power

The Power of Nurturing is born when we are born. It's usually at its most potent levels at that time. After all, babies can get grownups to feed, dress, and bathe them, change their diapers, play with them, cuddle, and get up in the middle of the night with specific directions. Yet those babies don't speak a word. At times, they nudge adults with a cry or two, but that's all it takes to get most grownups to quickly respond.

As we grow, we learn to play with the Power of Nurturing when we play with our dolls. We care for them temporarily, emulating how our parents took care of us. We feed them, get them new clothes, cover them at the end of the night, and leave them behind somewhere until the next playtime.

At this stage, girls are learning about their mothering power. Most importantly, they're learning how to mother themselves, which is the best use of this power.

As we mature, most of us diminish the level and intensity of our nurturing abilities, but it doesn't have to be that way. On the contrary, our power gains strength when we're able to communicate what we need from others and get our needs met. The Power of Nurturing isn't meant to give us fierce independence, although misinterpretations can lead to that. Instead, it's meant to bring us a balance between asking for support when we need it and taking steps to support ourselves when we're capable.

If we believe it's still someone else's job to give us what we need, we diminish the power and become dependent. Most of us tend to do an excellent job asking for what we want until we're about nine years old. Then, because of our conclusions based on the nurturing behaviors modeled for us, we become either independent warriors who refuse help, codependent victims who blame others, or good self-nurturing individuals. Of course, there are different levels of these three states of nurturing. But because the nurturing leakage begins after the age of nine, it would be wise to know where we reside most of the time on the spectrum.

Sometime after our ninth birthday, we have days when we mother ourselves well and some days when we don't. We begin to use our brains differently and create new behaviors that are the result of our conclusions about the people, things, and emotions we experienced in those nine years. Every unconscious decision begins to assert itself. Depending on the type of parents, teachers, and family members around us and the values they exposed to us, our decisions will support the development of the Nurturing Power or diminish it.

The Second Stage of Nurturing

During the second stage of the Nurturing Power, which begins around their first period, women start to play with their power in a different light. Things get a bit more challenging when we get our first menses. This is the day when our strong connection with our mothers begins to thin out. The link is still there, but nature silently whispers in girls' ears that the next stage of their nurturing begins. We must start mothering ourselves more consistently.

Most of the complexity has to do with our unconscious mind's notion of change. The mind doesn't like change. It wants to protect us from the unknown. But the status quo is death, and the mind needs to expand. This time is when you see a fourteen-year-old girl holding a boyfriend in her arms during the day and sleeping with dolls at night. She might cook for her girlfriends one day and be furious the next day that her parents didn't leave her any dinner.

Some of the challenges come from her mother's reaction to that change. Many mothers don't want the mother-daughter connection to thin out. They insist on keeping their daughters young, dependent, and controlled just like their mothers did with them. Other mothers want their daughters to gain more responsibilities, taking some of the mothering off their plates before the child is ready. Still, that initial independence/codependence will cause mothers to also fear the unknown.

In this state, women expand their capacity to nurture themselves and others. If girls feel safe, secure, and stable, they can navigate this stage well. That's when on random days, they choose to go to their rooms, have tea, or just read a book instead of hanging out with a friend. They also begin to feel that they have a solid footing in their life.

Girls who don't feel safe and secure and don't have stability early in their lives may have difficulty mothering themselves with nurturing behaviors, such as taking a nap, drinking water when thirsty, finding a quiet moment, saying no to friends, and other simple acts of self-care.

Also, girls who have to mother others early in their childhood will have difficulty nurturing themselves. This is because they're conditioned to mother others first instead of themselves. It sounds counterintuitive to say that children who mother other children and sometimes adults won't learn how to properly mother themselves. But one of the reasons children-mothers struggle to practice self-care is because when the natural nurturing powers are used earlier, their power is operated in depleted mode – a strong fight or flight pattern is set. These grown women are then likely to perceive self-nurturing as a burden because that's what it felt like to them when they had to be mothers to others before they were ready.

This early conditioning will lead them to care for others first and foremost, turning them into over-caregivers of others. Their instinctive reaction when they feel imbalanced, uncomfortable, or unvalidated is to give. Although helping others is always a lovely gesture, giving to others from that state of depletion is not soul-honoring.

It also sounds unfair that children who mother other children and adults would have a perceived disadvantage during their adult years. At first look, it may look like a drawback. However, when women are able to overcome their early beginnings by balancing their powers, they have the potential to reach higher nurturing powers than those who aren't. Let's not overlook the gift children-mothers receive by being born into families that need additional care. Not all is lost.

The great news is that when children-mothers reconcile their beginnings, realign their nurturing powers, and reprogram their perception from a burden to a gift, they become teachers of self-care. They know the non-self-nurturing behaviors in their bones, and when they're propelled to the opposite side, they reach mastery levels of the Power of Nurturing.

The Third Stage of Nurturing

The third stage of the Nurturing Power is when we embrace the power of mothering ourselves deeply, lovingly, and consciously first. We also begin to mother others, including our own mother, with a purpose. That's how we exercise the Power of Nurturing.

Some women enter this stage as early as the late twenties, and others don't reach it until much later. The process is called "conscious self-care." Some women are great at setting boundaries. They know how to say, "No, thank you," and when to ask for assistance. They expand this power by recharging with ease when they're called to give more. Other women have to learn, and we all learn differently.

Women awakening to the Power of Nurturing are taught best by their discontent with life. The universe constantly shows them what isn't nurturing so they can cross challenging situations off their list and look for better ones. Knowing what we don't want helps us know what we *do* want.

They can also learn from other women, classes, and books. However, the problem with learning how to practice the true Power of Nurturing from other women is that they may only recognize the power in mentors or very close friends. Otherwise, the nurturing practices may appear to them as selfish behaviors.

Learning from classes or books is good, but don't forget that the power already exists inside you. You really aren't learning but simply remembering. Certainly, women who recognize the need to improve self-care can use classes or books as a guide, but the daily practice of nurturing is the true game-changer. So, include activities in your day that strengthen your power.

One of the best practices of Nurturing Power is living in joy. Laugh and honor your spirit effortlessly in the name of happiness. If something brings you joy, say yes. If not, say no.

We also use the Power of Nurturing when we drink water regularly, sleep seven-plus hours at night, eat a good nutritious meal, embrace downtime, disconnect from doing things, and connect with ourselves. Women building their Nurturing Powers listen to their emotions and body. If you are too busy, you can't hear your feelings and your body.

Another characteristic of this third stage of nurturing is that we don't have complaints. There is no feeling of victimization coming from these lovely ladies who care for themselves and others without any feelings of burden or obligation. Of course, disappointments happen, but they don't invest their time in pity parties.

There is a Pause in the Period

Women are given a chance to exercise their Nurturing Power every month, arriving with our period.

My period arrived at age twelve, and I didn't tell my mother for two days. I don't know why. I knew what it was, but perhaps I didn't want to add another problem to the household. Here was another clue about inappropriate independence – you take on difficulties alone.

When I had my period, my mother, taught by her mother, instructed me to stay in the house during those red days. We lived in a two-bedroom apartment with eight people, and staying inside the house was a punishment for me. I was grounded quite often, so I wouldn't give up my freedom and stay home just to satisfy my period, mother, or grandmother. However, I suffered from cramps every month, so I had to stay home. The pain was so debilitating that my brothers, feeling sorry for me, brought buckets of warm water to soak my feet. That was a home remedy for cramps. Cramps are also a sign of chakra imbalance.

I hated having my period. By the time I was sixteen, I would go three to six months without having them. It didn't bother me at first until I started having sex. Then, it was stressful! Was I pregnant, or was it just another prank from my period for hating them?

When it did decide to visit me, the cramps would announce their arrival one day before the first drop, which meant I had to slow down. Then, it was a relief and a bit of depression.

Back then, I didn't realize that this time with myself during my period was necessary, and those downtimes helped me develop my Nurturing Powers. Many civilizations have considered a woman's monthly cycle both sacred and evil. Some cultures sought divination from women during their menses, while others allowed them to rest and not work. Still, others segregated women to separate quarters believing they were impure and evil.

In Nepal, a fifteen-year-old girl was banned from the house by her father for having her period and died from asphyxiation after lighting a fire to keep warm. The same sad death happened to a thirty-five-year-old mother and two young children when her husband sent her to the barn because she was impure. In Orthodox Jewish religion, women cannot return to their marital bed until they are purified after having a period. They immerse themselves in a mikvah bath to be sacred again. Although mikvah baths are now used for other rituals to mark milestones such as a birthday, bereavement, and recovery from divorce, the ancient belief that women are impure during their period is still practiced today.

The duality between the sacred and the evil could be interpreted as old superstitions. But what if a woman's cycle is a critical time? What if it's a reminder that our power is being renewed and recharged after being depleted? What if our cycles are nature's way of telling us it's time for self-care?

The human body is a sage. When women live in the same space, their cycles align with one another. When women genuinely connect with one another, they can create worlds. The energy level of the Power of Nurturing multiplied by the number of women in the same space can soothe and elevate the spirit of sisterhood rather than competition. It's almost like their spirits are whispering to each other, "I've got you."

Responsibilities That Come with the Power

As I said, the first purpose of the Nurturing Power is to mother ourselves. That's the most essential act of power and the reason to keep it in development. As the Nurturing Power fluctuates in strength, our ability to use it when needed is compromised.

The second function is to mother others through our relationships. Please understand that I don't mean we go around like super moms in red capes looking to mother everyone. We aren't professional rescuers. Instead, through our own nurturing, we help other people mother themselves. We may care for them temporarily, but they aren't our responsibility. That's what we do for our children and young people trusted to our care. We mother them until they can care for themselves, and we model healthy self-care behaviors.

Some women adopt pets, plants, causes, or projects instead of mothering other people. Having children is a personal choice, and there's nothing wrong with deciding not to become a mother, get married, or use your power for a cause, project, or animal. The only condition to this power is that you exercise your nurturing powers for yourself first before others, pets, projects, or causes.

Self-Care and Money

One sign that our nurturing powers are underpowered is a lack of money. When we don't have enough resources to pay our bills, feed our family, and enjoy life, the energy of our first chakra center is compromised. Do you have enough money to live a good life? If not, pay close attention to this section.

Nurturing energy helps us become grounded, which is a prerequisite for receiving abundance. When a woman is grounded, she feels her feelings, has a clear mind, knows what she wants to do, and can go about her day with ease. When a woman isn't grounded, she feels scattered, disconnected, forgetful, and discombobulated. Ungrounded women aren't able or willing to nurture themselves. It's like they're telling the universe, *See me through my eyes. I don't care about myself, and I don't deserve to have abundance.*

If you're a stay-at-home mother by choice, and I mean that you chose it for yourself, and your partner can't provide for your family, it's also a sign that your first power has been weakened. Even though you aren't the breadwinner, the Power of Nurturing is energy that revolves around you. And when you're just getting by financially, even though there's no lack, you're one emotion away from having more or having less.

But if you're struggling financially, please don't blame yourself or your partner. Your time is better spent embracing your ability to provide safety and security for you and your family.

I know that stay-at-home mothers work as much as working mothers, but perhaps you're being called to do more than raise your children. If your partner can't provide enough, you'll need to put your nurturing powers to work by finding a way to earn a living from home or taking on perhaps a part-time job outside the house. Traditional beliefs still dictate that women stay home and men go to work. But this is an archaic thought. More men are taking on the role of caring for children at home, while women are building their careers. More women and men are sharing the work and home life responsibilities. There is no one way. Today, you're called to exercise your nurturing power and find what is suitable and sustainable for you and your family.

As you read this chapter, you already know what to do because your heart is being opened. Perhaps you've been contemplating returning to work, getting a promotion with more responsibilities, or starting a part-time business. This is another nudge for you to take a step forward. If you're having a hard time getting out of bed, avoiding calls from collection agencies, or opening overdue bills, this is your wake-up call to stop blaming and waiting. Instead, begin to use your nurturing powers.

Women and money have been oxymorons for ages. The habit of allowing a partner to handle all financial affairs and not looking at money is an opportunity to begin exercising your Nurturing Powers there. I recommend that you read and listen to the work of Suze Orman and Leoni Dawson about money. These ladies have different approaches and styles toward money management and wealth, but they are aligned with the common intention of helping women find their powers in the area of money.

Nurturing Payoff

One of the best benefits of owning the Power of Nurturing is the increased resilience women get to experience. Nurtured women aren't afraid of failure. They tend to bounce back from disappointment, discouragement, and failure much faster than women who don't have a healthy nurturing practice. But women with high levels of Nurturing Powers actually don't fail. When they encounter setbacks, they know it and feel secure that it just wasn't the right time or that there's a better door for them to find.

In a study from the University of California-Berkeley, three groups of students were given a tough test designed to fail them, and everyone did fail. After the students received their results, one group was told not to worry about it because they were smart already since they got accepted into the university. It was meant to build their self-esteem. The second group was told nothing, and the third group was told to be compassionate with themselves because it happens to everyone.

The study found that people who were encouraged to be kind to themselves studied longer and tried harder for the next test. They also did better compared to the other two groups on the follow-up test. The people who were told nothing after the first test were likely to beat themselves up and not improve on the follow-up test. The group who received the pep talk showed some improvement, but it was based on the current level of self-esteem the students already possessed. Only individuals with self-esteem saw improvement.

People who are nurturing to themselves have the emotional resources to bounce back from failures. Of course, they get upset, but they're warm and encouraging toward themselves and have the resilience to begin again.

The School for Nurturing Powers

As I mentioned earlier, girls' mothering power begins to expand in the teen years. But, unfortunately, there is no proper schooling, nor will our mothers teach the skills. Life will teach us how to develop our powers through our relationships, regardless of our level of attention to them. But it helps to be aware of them and pay close attention.

The following questions will shine a light on the level of your Nurturing Power. Take three deep breaths, and answer each question honestly:

1) Do I feel I have a safe, secure, and clean place to live?
2) Does my partner or I pay all the bills on time monthly?
3) Does my partner or I have a job that can fully provide for my immediate family and me?
4) Do I feel safe and secure about my ability or my partner's ability to provide for our family?
5) Am I able to easily get out of bed, go to work, and contribute to life?
6) Am I able to purchase all the foods and supplies I need?
7) Do I feel I receive the emotional, physical, and spiritual support I need?
8) Do I take the time to rest and play?
9) Do I eat, drink water, and sleep regularly?
10) Does the care I provide for others – people, pets, projects – not deplete my energy?

If you answered yes to eight or more questions, you're doing great with your Nurturing Power.

If you answered yes to five or more questions, you need to energize your Nurturing Power

If you answered yes to four or fewer questions, you need to rebuild your Nurturing Power.

Pay close attention to the next segment and make notes of the insights you receive.

How to Rebuild Your Nurturing Power

Here are four ways to awaken and rebuild your Nurturing Power, get the right footing in life to handle anything that comes your way, and ground yourself to create and receive abundance.

One – Mothering Yourself

The quickest and best way to awaken and renew your Nurturing Power is through mothering yourself. Sounds simple, right? Not so fast. If you haven't been able to mother yourself in the past, you have to become the kind of mother you need at this moment. What kind of mother does a motherless woman need? One who is loving and kind, even if you have a great mother in reality.

The late Louise Hay, author and teacher, said that we need to be patient with ourselves. So, as you begin to awaken the Power of Nurturing, you'll be able to do it with ease most days. Other days, you'll default to your old ways. You must be patient.

Pay attention to the way you talk to yourself. You're either lifting yourself up or beating yourself down. If you find yourself being a demanding mother to yourself, acknowledge it, release the thought, and mindfully affirm the type of mother you want to be.

The intent is to feel safe and secure like the first feelings of safety and security we receive from our mothers. Can you be patient, loving, and kind to yourself right now? Ask yourself, *if I was going to be kind to myself now, what would I do?*

Could you give yourself a hug? Cross your arms, and with your hands, caress your upper arms as you take a long and slow breath. Also, please caress your head, shoulders, and chest as you say to yourself, "I love you" multiple times. Try it. Don't hesitate. Do it now. Put the book down, and give yourself the love and kindness you're craving from your mother. You can be your mother at this moment, the next, and the next.

Practice this short exercise several times daily for at least three minutes each time. You're working with the body-mind code. Your body will recognize the earliest signal of mothering you had and respond appropriately. It's very simple, but it works fast. Remember that you are a powerful woman. These actions will slow you down enough to be grounded.

Two – Practicing Forgiveness

To continue to be the kind of mother you need now, you must forgive yourself. People who have low mothering skills tend to be hard on themselves. Use the feeling of forgiveness for everything you feel you didn't do well. Remember that you're now a kind and loving mother to yourself. Perhaps you've neglected yourself through your eating and sleeping habits. Maybe you've criticized yourself for the things you didn't do, the mistakes you've made, and the choices you didn't have full awareness to make. Go ahead and forgive yourself. You only did what you could have done based on the level of awareness you had at that time.

Also, you may need to forgive your mother. Some people may not be ready to do that because they have a list of unfit qualities running through their heads. Let's retitle that list as "My Expectations of My Mother." This is the list you created for someone else to be. Everyone has the right to choose to be who they want to be. This doesn't mean it's right to abandon, mistreat, or abuse a child. But bad things sometimes happen for many reasons.

If it happened to you, I am very sorry for your pain. I am sorry for the days you hoped things to be different, and nothing happened. I am sorry for your feelings about your mother, but I am also glad you got here. There is relief on the other side of this mountain.

Today is the day when you forgive her. You aren't agreeing with her actions. You understand that her choices hurt you, and those choices will be her own cross to bear. But please don't judge her through the lenses of hurt and victimization. You won't win, and she won't lose either. Right now, you can make a decision to no longer carry her burden. You can let go of the cross and not increase the weight with your thoughts of anger, revenge, and even hate. You can let it all go.

You are practicing forgiveness for yourself, not for her, because resentment weighs on your soul. A good mindful practice for forgiveness is to write down on paper a list of all the expectations you created for your mother. Write down everything you believe she *should* have done but didn't. Take three deep breaths, and then read each sentence out loud. At the end of each sentence, add, "And I forgive you for it."

It will look like this:

You never call … (And I forgive you for it.)
You abandoned me … (And I forgive you for it.)
You criticize me all the time … (And I forgive you for it.)

Once you're done with your list of forgiving, and you've released any tears and emotions, flush the list down the toilet or burn it outdoors. See the water or the smoke remove the heavy feelings from your body. Wait three days, and tune into your feelings about your mother again. Check if your resentment has dissipated or diminished considerably. If not, do the practice again.

Remember to let the tears fall. Women release unwanted energy through their tears. You're going to be okay. You are now your own mother who doesn't hold on to resentment.

Three – Build a Practice of Self-Care

When you're being a good mother to yourself, you tend to give yourself what you need. If you don't have a good self-care practice, I recommend starting with the basics. If you're thirsty, drink water. If you're hungry, eat good foods. If you're tired, go to bed. You'll be surprised how many women forget to drink water – and we need six to eight glasses a day! Drink that much for one week, and see what it does for your skin, energy, and understanding of self-care. Also, food and rest are top priorities for a powerful woman.

By starting my day with two glasses of water, I've learned that I'm very likely to reach the eight glasses by the end of the day. Also, planning my meals for several days makes me more likely to eat healthily and not forget to eat.

You can also improve your self-care by managing your relationships. Spend more time with people you love and who uplift you. Eliminate the time you spend with negative people who deplete your energy. If you feel obligated to spend time with family members who don't inspire you, minimize your time with them. The holidays can be a bit tricky, as our families expect us to give up our freedom and be miserable with some of them. Do yourself a favor, and don't give them health excuses like the flu. Instead, say, "We decided to have a unique Thanksgiving, and we won't make it." Don't elaborate. If they ask additional questions, say, "I don't want to jinx it." Send a huge basket of fruit to them and be done with it. There may be some drama, but it isn't your drama. As you build your Power of Nurturing, what other people think of you isn't your problem, and it will bother you less and less.

Four – Listen to the Nine Powers Meditation

Another form of self-care is done through meditation, which can help you tune into your higher self, create a pause in your day, rebuild your health, and give you insights into your life and heal your nervous system. Yes, people who are not grounded may have an active nervous system that stops them from relaxing and sleeping well.

What I love about meditation the most is that it helps you stay within your power and gives you the tools to stay balanced, less reactive, and focused on what you want to do. This is one way to ground your energy.

The Nine Powers of Women Meditation begins with a body-mind code. I ask you to lean against a solid surface, face the main door to the room, and feel your back against the wall or a pillow. Then, I invite you to feel your buttocks against the surface you are sitting on. The body-mind connection to feel safety and support is in our DNA. In ancient times, our safety depended on us looking at the entrance to our cave and having a solid surface against our backs so that we wouldn't fall asleep. Our support comes from the ground, our mother earth. This practice alone will help you feed energy into your first energy center: the root chakra. This energy is responsible for your ability to get out of bed, go to work, and provide for yourself and your family. If you think about Maslow's Hierarchy of Needs, this practice infuses energy for the first two human needs: food and shelter, followed by safety and security.

The second part of the meditation will work with your own energy power or QI, pronounced "chi," also called your life force. This is done through your breath. We'll use your breath to awaken the first energy center, infuse your life force, and open the essence of your center's energy. So, it isn't just a spiritual practice but also a practical tool. The meditation will work with all nine powers.

As you begin to feel safe, your energy will rise. When you feel supported, cared for, and loved, you'll activate your reticular activating system in your brain. This system will help you pay attention to the abundance of opportunities you'll attract with your renewed intention of mastering the Power of Nurturing. Pay close attention because you will begin to receive ideas, hear suggestions from friends, receive job offers, have more downtime, and discover many solutions for the current conditions that don't support a woman with high levels of Nurturing Power. You can do it!

Here are some of the signs that you're growing and exercising your Nurturing Power:

- You feel safe in your home, your job, and your relationships.
- You're able to clean the house, cook meals, and take long breaths.
- You have the financial resources to pay your bills, buy food, and take time off.
- You start earning more money unexpectedly and have more cash leftover.
- You eat well, drink water daily, move every day, and sleep well each night.

Pull out your journal or the *Nine Powers of Women Book Companion* and list the actions you plan to take to begin practicing more nurturing behaviors.

Women who practice the Power of Nurturing are woven voracious energy of self-care and self-love in humanity through the rooms of their lives. Men and women will be influenced by extraordinary women who care for themselves as a loving and kind mother would. These powerful ladies build a safety blanket in their homes, work, and communities. Feeling safe is the key foundation for every beginning. We teach what we have to learn. Keep adding to the humanity blanket; it's calling for cooperation and kindness.

Chapter 2
The Power of Creativity

"Creativity is intelligence having fun."

— ALBERT EINSTEIN

The second power every woman has is the Power of Creativity. It's the power used to give birth to something new in the world, such as a baby, a book, a painting, a meal, or a new way of living. This power gives women the ability to be imaginative, create something brand new, or transform something old.

The Power of Creativity is connected to the second energy center of the body, which is located just behind the belly button and called the sacral chakra. This is a significant power center because it gives us the ability to create a life worth living. It's energized by the color orange and the element of water.

Creating our lives is the primary use of our Power of Creativity. We use this power with our imagination. Every time you imagine anything, you're being creative. And when we create a wonderful life, it magnifies that possibility for the people we attract into our lives.

When you hear people say that they aren't creative, it's only because they aren't tuned into their wisdom. Everyone has the Power of Creativity, with no exceptions. When you cut your hair, buy new clothes, select a paint color for the bedroom, plant flowers in the garden, cook a meal, wear new jewelry, you are being creative. The power may be dormant or reduced, but only because the individual is disconnected from their inner self.

People who believe they aren't creative made a conscious or unconscious decision to not believe in their ability. They likely made a drawing as a child, compared it with someone else's picture, and then concluded that they weren't creative. The worst part is that their minds believed their early conclusions.

Take a slow and deep breath now and look at your life. Look at your home, job, friends, and experiences. This is the life you created. If you like what you see, you're doing a great job using your creative power. If you don't like how your life looks and feels, it means you aren't using your creative power intentionally, at least to the best of your potential. This just means you need some help developing this power.

Pause now and take note of everything you believe your life needs to be. Use your book companion or write it down in your journal.

(PAUSE)

Did you envision your life as you wanted? Or did you think of everything that you don't like? If you listed the things that don't belong in the life you want, you just moved toward creating what you *don't* want. If you can't think of what you want, you're creating without intention. You're setting your life up to be influenced by the news or any upsets you experience in your day-to-day life. If you encounter happy events, your creations will be happy ones, but you're still leaving them to chance.

Creating starts by imagining what you *do* want. Leave out what you don't like, and concentrate on the positive images in your mind.

You may be a little puzzled when you take a current life inventory. Perhaps you believe you inherited the life you have by chance or that you were a victim of unforeseen circumstances. Or you may even think that there's no way out of the mess you see yourself in. Although it makes you feel better to believe you are a trapped victim, not taking authorship for your life robs you of the Power of Creativity and doesn't serve you. Furthermore, feeling like a victim robs you of the possibility of changing your life for the better.

Let's look at the huge role the Power of Creativity plays in your life. Every time you cook, plant something, decorate, write, clean your home, and do the thousands of activities you do every month, you put your stamp on your life. You're creating your world. Every idea you have consciously or unconsciously causes you to create. Every moment in life is the result of your thoughts manifested. The combination of all things you think, feel, do, or don't do build the life you have. That's both good news and bad news. The bad news is that some of the thoughts weren't aligned with the life you desire, and the good news is that not every idea you have comes to fruition.

In the same way, positive thoughts can create an amazing life. It all depends on your ability to focus your creative force on accomplishing the things you believe will make you happy instead of focusing on things that won't.

Inspiration

Many of us have been conditioned to pay attention to what's missing in our life. That results in two significant setbacks when it becomes a habit. One, we create what we don't want. After some time, we become accustomed to lacks and disappointments. And two, we create without inspiration. We can't look for failures all the time and see possibilities. It's counter-intuitive, and that isn't how our brain works. We need to see the glass half full or at least a quarter full, instead of three-quarters empty. That's what inspiration does for us.

I like to think of inspiration as a magic potion. You tap into inspiration, and you color your life. Inspiration literally means "being in spirit." It's a beautiful emotion to experience. Creating from inspiration shows that you're aligned with a higher power—the best part of you. When you're "in spirit," you experience deep emotions of love, connection, ecstasy, hope, and the feel-good experiences that the poets, composers, and writers attempt to describe in their work.

So how do you find that inspiration? You don't find it. You become it. And you don't need to be an artist to do that.

As children, we're open to inspiration in every moment. Like a breeze that flows through the window, the inspiration that always existed goes from invisible to action. Then, suddenly, a brown cardboard box becomes a castle, a truck, or a cave. Where did our inspiration go? It didn't go anywhere. It's all around us, waiting to connect with our Creative Power.

If you aren't happy with your life, you can be sure that you aren't connecting with inspiration. I suspect that the cardboard boxes won't do it for you anymore. It may have become foreign to you. But don't despair; there are many ways for you to reconnect with the same emotion that delighted you at the possibility of building a castle made of cardboard boxes. That inspiration will create the life you desire.

It's very likely that you look at successful people and wonder how they do it. Some people seem to have immense inspiration behind their creative power. Look at J. K. Rowling, the author of the *Harry Potter* books. Her creativity is off the charts. Not only has she created an imaginative world, but she also created a life for herself beyond her wildest dreams.

Before becoming a famous writer, Rowling was broke, unemployed, and living on welfare as a single mother. She wrote the first book in a coffee shop with her young daughter sleeping next to her. Inspiration struck while riding the train, and it took her five years to fully develop the characters and write the story. She battled depression and received many rejection letters from publishers before someone finally agreed to publish it. So how did she do it? Keep reading to understand how the creative power works.

How Does Creative Power Translate in Your World?

Vincent Van Gogh, who created more than two thousand paintings and sketches during a ten-year period as a painter, said that he dreamed of his paintings and then painted his dreams. He sold only one artwork while he was alive. After his death, his work awarded him the reputation of the greatest post-Impressionist of the century, inspiring other artists to continue their own work.

As I've said, however, the Power of Creativity isn't just for musicians, painters, sculptors, and writers. It has been responsible for all sorts of innovations, scientific advancements, new discoveries, expansion of consciousness and thought, abundance, amusement, and more. It's an act of expression that calls each individual to share their uniqueness with the world.

The Power of Creativity is constantly expanding. When a woman cooks a quick meal with a few leftovers, redecorates the bedroom, or plants flowers in the garden, she uses her Power of Creativity. When scientists discover a new vaccine or a businesswoman starts a new company, they also use the same creative power.

It can be exercised in any intensity, time, or space. It depends on your beliefs, the level of soul connection to inspiration, and the desire for expression. These conditions will determine how vibrant the creative power is exercised in your life. If you don't believe you can create your world or tap into your pool of inspiration, that belief will stand in your way. I've found that many women exercise their creative power inside their heads, but they avoid the moment of actually expressing it. However, if they connect with inspiration, they will be pulled by the need to express it effortlessly, regardless of whatever fears they feel.

Creativity is a yin power that calls for yang energy so that it can be expressed. Remember the white dot on the dark yin? Creativity is the perfect subject to help us understand how yin and yang energy go together.

All great ideas in your head (yin) gain traction when they connect with the energy of implementation and construction (yang). The world is full of people with millions of ideas to transform their world but no initiative to make the ideas a reality. Strong inspiration can be the propeller to move creativity out of our heads and into the world.

Creativity is also the power we use to solve problems. People with a good level of creativity take more time to solve problems because they have faith they'll find a way. Conversely, people who believe they have low creativity tend to give up on the first obstacle.

Women's Creativity

Although there is a tremendous bias against women and creativity, and both men and women believe that men are more creative than women, science could not confirm it outside individual judgments and the association of creativity to male traits. However, a study by Columbia Business School found that estrogen is the culprit in finding that women are more creative than men. Estrogen is a sex hormone found in males and females, but females have higher estrogen levels than males. Our yin energy supports the ability to flow with ideas. History took care of having space for women to be creative, at least in part because we were obligated for so long to be passive. But when women had great ideas, they weren't allowed to take ownership of those ideas.

Today's society may not perceive the high levels of creativity of women. It's a huge disappointment for our gender and a loss of great talent. When we measure the gap between what women endured in the past and where we are today, creativity played a huge role in our advancement. Women organized in hiding and created opportunities with limited resources. Many women over the centuries had to impersonate men to make it through.

Jazz musician Billy Tipton was born Dorothy Lucille Tipton, a beautiful and talented musician who was turned down until she impersonated a man. The English novelist Mary Shelley, the author of *Frankenstein*, wanted to remain anonymous when she published her first books. However, many assumed her husband Percy Bysshe Shelley had written *Frankenstein* because he wrote a preface for the book. Even today, critics still believe Mary's husband wrote the book; they believed that a woman couldn't have written that great of a story. Kathrine Switzer competed in the Boston Marathon in

1967 under K.V. Switzer because women weren't allowed to enter the race. Joanne Rowling also used the pen name J.K. Rowling because female authors would be less likely to make it in a target audience of young boys.

History is full of creative women who were largely forgotten because of social inequality. Many of the ones who made enormous contributions while openly female were far from celebrated at the time. Women like Katherine Johnson, an African-American mathematician who did crucial work for NASA by fixing the calculations that got the first man on the moon; Emily Warren Roebling, the woman behind the completion of the Brooklyn Bridge after her husband died; and Reverend Pauli Murray, an African-American lawyer, Feminist, Activist, Poet who relentlessly laid the groundwork for fighting gender and race-based discrimination. These and many other women were not recognized for their efforts until recently.

I invite you to change the history we are creating today.

Although many will agree that women are being more creative these days, we have yet another obstacle to conquer: interruptions. Women are the primary caretakers and often the breadwinners too. We are being pulled in many directions to provide support to our tribe. Where is the time to create? One of the biggest problems women find today when creating is interruptions by children, spouses, parents, friends, and work. Technology reduced the space between solitude and connection. The writer Joyce Carol Oates advises women writers to run away and write because interruptions kill creativity. We must disconnect to tap into our creative flow.

Since I was very young, I loved the loneliness of the house when everyone was at church, and I was home alone with a fever. What a quiet companion. The weekends my children visited their father became a sanctuary even when I cleaned, cooked, did laundry, and met my bed exhausted at the end of the day. There were no questions to answer or obligations to attend to. Women must have time to dream about their creations.

The Balance of Power

The Power of Creativity needs to be balanced. When it's well-adjusted, women can have fun, laugh at themselves, tap into inspiration, invite ideas, and see them to fruition. Their lives may not be all roses, but they're satisfied with the experiences they create as they see fit.

If the Power of Creativity is in overdrive, many ideas will flourish, but nothing will likely get created. With too many ideas, the energy is dissipated, and there isn't enough life force to get them off the ground. When this power is overactive for long periods of time, women also tend to ignore their sexuality. All of their creative juice goes to the creative project, and nothing else matters.

Artists, executives, or PTA moms who immerse themselves into their work for long periods often find their creative power in overdrive. As a result, they ignore food, water, sleep, and sex until they exit the "creative zone" – the time where their creativity is heightened. They might even find physical relief in substance abuse, such as drugs, alcohol, or food.

On the other hand, substance abuse is also a risk when this power is underactive or dormant. Women with underactive creativity may believe that creativity isn't in their cards. They may be discontent with their careers and relationships. They need time and space in their environment, mind, and spirit in order to create.

In my first book, *Women, Rice, and Beans*, I talked about the need for women to have a space of their own. I call it a Sacred Space. This space could be an empty room, but it may not be a reality for most. An area in the house or a chair in a corner will be enough for women to connect with their spirits. We must recharge if we want to be helpful to ourselves or anyone else. These times of rest are great opportunities for us to connect with our inspiration. Many of my ideas come from those spaces during or after meditation.

Sometimes, artists find themselves stuck creatively. They can't write a sentence, select a paint color, write a song, or walk into their studio to create. This is a sign of underactive power. At the end of this chapter, I will share my suggestions for riding the waves of lack of creativity and getting your groove back.

Time Off is Not a Luxury

Your creativity can be infused with power any time you disconnect from stress. Turning off your phone and unplugging the computer can be an excellent way to get the inspiration flowing.

As women, we must be able to disconnect from work, and that includes even stay-at-home moms. If at all possible, taking a few days away from the children will help you become a better parent. Disconnecting from work will help you be a happy worker. We must give our Power of Creativity the room to wander and dream. New experiences such as going on vacation can be a great way to invest energy in your creative power. But if that isn't possible for you right now, do everything you can to give yourself a break, even if only a few hours. Maybe trade-off with another mom to take her kids for a few hours while she gets a break and vice versa.

But try not to do staycations too frequently. I've learned that it takes a day or two to disconnect from work when you go on vacation. If you stay home, you'll likely notice all of the little projects that need to be completed, so you will not rest. You're better off going to your in-laws than staying home. Any incomplete project in their house is *theirs*, not yours.

Of course, cashing in your vacation time may not be the best decision for you. If you need money, use your creativity to find ways to get more money so that you can have the downtime you need to access your inspiration.

But if you can afford it, take a vacation to visit new places. Let your senses be surprised by what you discover. You'll return inspired and with renewed creative power.

The School for Creative Power

Creativity is very high during the first nine years of our development. During that time, we have tremendous curiosity. We have the desire to create what we are beginning to imagine.

The adults around us weren't schooled in how to maintain our creative powers, however. Often, our imagination is discouraged as we age. Some parents and teachers believe that being realistic is the best way to live. The idea that we must face reality, bite the bullet, and work hard to overcome the inevitable struggles in life is far from the best way to encourage inspiration. These attitudes are counterproductive. In an attempt to avoid disappointment, which is the only reason to be a realist, we cut our connection with creativity and inspiration.

Creativity and inspiration lighten our lives. They color our perceptions and build hope and enthusiasm. These emotions lead the body to produce hormones that promote health and help regenerate the body. Cutting ties with imagination is a high price to pay just to become a realist, which could also be called a pessimist since they are preparing for the worse.

What is Your Creative Level?

The following questions will shine a light on the level of your creativity. Take three deep breaths, and answer:
1) Do I feel creative?
2) Do I do anything creative in my life?
3) Do I have room for creativity in my work?
4) Do I believe I created my life?
5) Am I happy with the life I created?
6) Do I laugh often?
7) Do I have time and space to express my creativity?
8) Do I enjoy food and alcohol in moderation?
9) Do I enjoy sex regularly?
10) Do I feel my workload is fair?

If you answered yes to eight or more questions, you're doing great with your creative power.

If you answered yes to five or more questions, you need to energize your creative power.

If you answered yes to four or fewer questions, you need to rebuild your creative power.

Take notes about the insights you receive in the next section.

The Body, Mind, & Wisdom School: How Do You Improve the Power of Creativity?

Every woman wants to have a good level of creative power. Here are six ways for you to improve your power.

One – Laugh Your Behind Off

An easy way to awaken the Power of Creativity is by laughing. Laugh until your tummy hurts and you fall on the floor, saying, "Stop!" You could rent a few Netflix comedy shows or watch funny clips on YouTube. Laughing is the equivalent of two thousand chocolates in your brain. If your power is dormant or underactive, go ahead and binge on comedy. Laughing will dust off the second energy center and give you the boost to be creative and transform the aspects of your life that need change.

Two – Become a Child of Picasso

Another way to exercise your creative power is to do something artistic, even if your DNA screams, "I'm *not* artistically inclined!" Take a painting, drawing, sculpture, or poetry class, and refrain from judging your work. You aren't training to be a Picasso or a Michelangelo. You're just expressing a glimpse of your creative power. This energy will infuse your life with fun.

Three – Tune into HGTV

Bring out your decorator's hat and change a room in your house. You can browse magazines for ideas and inspiration to pump up your creativity, or you can just do what you like. You aren't copying anything; you're modeling after it and making it your own. If you choose to redecorate your bedroom, you'll double your creative energy. That's because every energy intention in the bedroom will impact the people who sleep in it. Also, small accents in orange will energize your creativity (if you like the color). But *don't paint a whole room orange.* This powerful color is perfect for an accent, but too much can lead people to overeat, abuse alcohol and drugs, and binge TV, which ultimately diminishes their energy.

A little Feng Shui tip for you: the excessive use of the color orange is more intense when it's the first color you see when you enter the home or sleep in it. So a little will go a long way.

Four – Dream Up Your Life

At the beginning of this chapter, I called your attention to the life you created for yourself. If you aren't happy with your life, change it. How? Begin by dreaming it instead of complaining. Envision how you want your life to be. You can create vision boards by using pictures from magazines representing the type of life you want to live. Don't worry about how you're going to make it happen; just dream away and dream often. The problem that most people encounter is that they don't know what they want in life. They often complain about what they don't have, but they can't see in their minds what it could be.

So put the book down, close your eyes, and imagine where you would most like to live, what time you would get up, how you would spend your days, what activities would make you very happy. What type of work would you do? Where would you go on vacation? Who would you spend time with? Then feel the feelings you'll have when this is your life. The keyword here is to *feel.* Feel the emotions you know you will feel when your dreams are realized.

Do this exercise a few times a day and see how your vision changes over the course of a week. It will become more consistent with time. And if you catch yourself thinking of what you don't want, stop! Then, begin again with the life you *do* want. Also, pay attention to the opportunities showing up at your steps. Pay attention to the inklings you are called to. Sometimes those calls will repeat themselves until you hear them. Keep looking for the openings of the universe. This will distract you from your complaints.

It may seem like a waste of time to imagine a life you don't see as possible yet, but once your vision becomes consistent and you can feel happy with your imagination alone, the universe will find ways to create the best version of your vision for you. Your job is to just imagine, pay attention, and go with the flow.

Five – Immerse Yourself in Inspiration

The best use of your creative power is to create the life of your dreams. If you don't know what lifts your heart, you need to connect with the energy of inspiration. Go for a walk in a green space you enjoy. Being in nature will reduce your connection with beta waves (the energy that makes you overthink) and get you into alpha or gamma waves (the energy that connects with your heart and your inner world). Perhaps a long drive without a destination and without traffic would be helpful. Your mind tends to wander while driving. Make a conscious commitment to remember the good things instead of what's missing. Play your favorite music and feel the music in your memory and body. Remember what made you happy in the past, and milk that feeling. This will ease you into inspiration.

Six – Practice Mindfulness

Another way to create your life is by practicing mindfulness. It will stop you from creating life by default if you have negative expectations. Find the time and space where you can give yourself about fifteen minutes of uninterrupted time. Sit comfortably in a chair, on a bed, or on a pillow. Close your eyes. You can play meditation music if you like while you take at least thirty-three slow, deep breaths, or you can listen to a guided meditation of seven minutes or more. Then, open your eyes, and answer these three questions:

1) What is right about my life? (List everything great about your life.)
2) What do I need to see/experience/feel more in my life? (Build it from what you already have.)
3) How do I envision my life to be? (Be wild with your imagination.)

While you were answering these three questions, your brain took you in another direction. You were shown glimpses of things in the back of your mind. They were brief, passing thoughts. Did you catch them? Perhaps you thought about moving, leaving your job, starting a business, or writing a book. Pay attention to them. These are insights. Often, they remind you of the actions you've needed to take but have been hesitant about. Maybe you're fearful. Write down your insights.

What Side Do You Lean Towards?
(A quick exercise)

You must fall in love with the future you are creating. Inspiration will always trump any fear you have. Try this short exercise to check if you are sponsoring fear or possibilities:

Stand up. Keep your eyes open. Put your arms out. Imagine that you're standing on the top of a wall, carrying a bag of sand in each hand. In the left hand, the bag represents your current life. On the right hand, the bag represents the life you want. Think about your vision and imagine yourself walking on the wall. Keep imagining the life you have and the life you want.

Now, close your eyes, and in your mind's eye, see yourself walking on the wall. Then, run on the wall. As you run, the wall gets narrower and narrower. Finally, you're about to fall. Which side do you fall on, the left or the right? If you fall to the left side, you still need to build your life through imagination. If you fail to the right, you're going in the right direction.

Closing Thoughts

Remember, you need to tap into your yang energy to bring your ideas into form. You can do that now by assigning one action to the top two ideas you came up with to create the life you want to live. You must do one action within twenty-four hours. Then, another within forty-eight hours. These can be small actions such as writing them down on paper, researching online, etc.

If you have too many ideas, pick two. The best way to know if you're aligned with your thoughts is by closing your eyes, placing your dominant hand on the center of your throat, and asking questions about the idea. You will have a feeling, a thought, or even hear a response. This is your inner guidance. Follow it!

Doing this will create momentum, and momentum is your best friend when creativity is a concern.

IDEA #1: _____

ACTION 1: _____

ACTION 2: _____

IDEA #2: _____

ACTION 1: _____

ACTION 2: _____

Once you have taken two actions, you can keep asking yourself what's next. If you fall in love with the life you want to create, the following steps will be shown to you. Remember, you are not thinking of the steps, only the end results – what your life will look like.

By imagining the life you want and feeling the feelings of your future life, the following action will be effortless. The Power of Creativity will help you fully understand that *life is a journey*, not a destination. Be prepared to be amazed by your ongoing creations.

Women who practice the Power of Creativity become very happy women. It seems that when they walk, they leave traces of little dancing stars flowing like rainbows after a rainstorm. Most of us don't quite know what to make of it; we just become engaged and invested by their light. We love a creative woman. They are open. It's like they carry fairy dust the wind sprinkled in her house, work, and community. We wonder if her voice, touch, and air have magic. We leave them mesmerized by their breath. Be open to becoming a strong creative woman.

HELP ME! I'm a Stuck Artist

It seems to me that every artist goes through a period where they aren't creating. After a few weeks, artists who depend on their work to support them financially begin to panic. Many tend to abuse alcohol, drugs, coffee, cigarettes, and/or food within a few weeks. So, what seems to be a lack of creativity is only space for higher levels of inspiration to be downloaded.

The strategies I've suggested to improve your creativity will work, but they may not be the best option for you if you're called to higher levels of creation. It will get you producing, but the results may not be your best work.

To get out of the funk, first follow my six suggestions in this chapter. If you're unable to tap into your creative flow, then I invite you to ride the wave.

Think of the ocean. It's immense. No one can tell where it begins and where it ends. Now, think of the waves. You can see the ups and the downs, and they're an extension of the whole ocean.

The creative power is like the waves. They're part of an immense scheme and show up in surges—some big, some small. You can listen to the sounds of the waves or go to the ocean to see and hear them in person.

When your creative juice is low, ride the wave. I want you to know that the high wave is coming. It has to. This alone will reduce your anxiety and stress, enabling you to get ready to ride the waves of creativity. For those hours or days, allow the wave to be. You can rest in your office or studio, close your eyes, and see the waves. Breathe with the pattern of the waves. Breathe in the crest and breathe out the trough. Play the waves sound and become one with them.

This practice connects you with the energy field that's all around, which is where your creativity resides. Yes, your ability to create is all around, but you're just in the wrong frequency because of your thoughts or feelings. Sometimes, you need to step out of the usual energy to learn, grow, and be open to what is next.

Science has shown that detaching from the status quo helps you be more creative. Many professional writers and painters have the discipline to sit at their desks or canvas five days a week, six to eight hours a day and create week after week. Some will demand the inspiration to come every morning at 8 a.m., and the work appears. Because the work is flowing, the feeling of relief leads them to tap into the field of creativity and continue to create. They are not riding the wave; they are communing with the ocean.

Relax and allow your power to express its flow. You're in charge of creating, and you reside in the field of creativity. All you need is to connect to it. You are the flow.

Chapter 3
The Power of Confidence

*"No one can make you feel inferior
without your consent."*

— ELEANOR ROOSEVELT

The third Power of Women is the Power of Confidence. This power is connected to the third energy center of the body located just in the center of your stomach below your breasts. It's the area we call our gut, which is also the home of our willpower and self-trust. In the East, it's called the solar plexus chakra. This center is energized by the color yellow and the fire element.

Before we dive into the Power of Confidence, however, I would ask you to set aside everything you believe about your confidence. I intend to disrupt the myths you may have heard about women and confidence.

Confidence is one of the most needed of the Nine Powers of Women.

For thousands and thousands of years, women were told they were unimportant. Revered scholars promoted the idea that women had low value in society. Religion also strengthened those beliefs in the minds and hearts of both sexes.

Over the centuries, women had to work twice as hard to do the simple things we take for granted today, such as voting, working, securing fair pay, getting a divorce, or even having a bank account or owning property. There is no doubt that history has conditioned women to think less of themselves and their abilities. We were surrounded by authority figures who commanded women to take an invisible place in society.

Today, I ask that you spend your time awakening your power of confidence because you are needed. Humanity needs you. And, still, there is a lot of work we need to do to repair the consciousness of women and men about the vital role women carry in our homes, communities, religious organizations, schools, corporations, boardrooms, and governments. Today, you're called upon to honor your gender in the way it was always intended—to uplift the world, balance power, and preserve humanity.

The Superpower

I call the Power of Confidence our superpower. A little dose of confidence will go a long way. Every girl begins to develop a level of confidence around her third birthday, no exceptions. I love seeing girls build their assertiveness during the third year of their life. These young ladies show great curiosity when asking questions; they also cry when they can't get their way and tend to wander and impose themselves on everyone's attention.

Although we don't call that energy "confidence" in three-year-old girls, it's vital energy for women down the road. Girls can flourish when they're encouraged to hold their curiosity and certainty in their home environment. Conversely, when gender expectations are imposed with statements like "girls don't do that," the Power of Confidence diminishes its capacity to grow and be exercised as intended.

Typically, from childhood on, the confidence level in women seems to diminish. I suspect that our society's rules begin to trim our confidence level at an early age. We learn bias behaviors: boys do this, and girls do that. Perhaps it's unintentional. However, most of us aren't aware of our inherited prejudices against girls. By pure osmosis, girls and boys grow with the hidden notion that women are weak beings. It has been happening for thousands of years. It isn't true, and we can change this erroneous perception today. But it requires that women and men change their biased perceptions and that women grow their confidence level.

When I say that every woman has confidence, I often hear, "If every woman has a good level of confidence, where is mine? How come I can't act with confidence?" Many of us don't know how to connect with that feeling. We wish we could see, touch, and smell it the same way we experience love or happiness. Actually, we know how, but we have forgotten because we don't believe we have it.

The Power of Confidence is a sense, a belief in our ability to succeed. It's an emotion. That's why no one but yourself can use your confidence. It belongs to you alone. This power is hidden in your subconscious, and it is inside of you right now.

Sometime between the ages of three and ten, you decided about your confidence. It was likely an unconscious decision to keep you safe. Of course, your environment had a huge influence on what you chose. Your home life, school, friendships, and television guided you in processing how confident you could be in that space. I've found that women with low confidence levels usually experienced a traumatic event during that age span that led them to believe they couldn't venture out of their comfort zone. Most of those who did were met with disapproval.

On the other side, women with high confidence levels were often encouraged and supported when they ventured beyond the pale.

Many people aren't aware of the traumas they experienced that caused them to lose confidence. From an adult perspective, it might not look like trauma at all, but from a child's perspective, it was very traumatic indeed.

A simple way to find the trauma is to bring to mind a situation that elicits anxiety. Perhaps it's a job interview, a tough conversation you need to have with your spouse, asking for job advancement, or just going on a date. Bring the situation to mind, close your eyes, and feel where you experience the anxiety in your body. Then, depending on where the discomfort is located, you can narrow down the year when it happened. For example, if you feel it in the heart area, it likely occurred when you were four. If you feel it in your throat, it probably happened when you were five. We can identify the age range because traumas get lodged in the energy centers that are in development at the time. This is a great system! Because we're usually too young to remember the events, the seven main energy centers will hold the trauma in energy form and help us overcome it. Because the body needs expression and expansion, similar events will repeat seven, fourteen, or twenty-one years later in multiples of seven. Other times, our body will give us clues that energy is stuck in one of the centers with a disease, that are imbalances in the body. At those times, we will have the opportunity to transcend and transmute the energy that doesn't serve us.

Confidence or lack of confidence is energy that cannot be destroyed. This emotion will live in the solar plexus center of the body until transmuted. So, around our tenth, seventeenth, and twenty-fourth years (multiples of seven after the third birthday), we will attract events that trigger us to open our energy center and let the energy run free, doing what it's supposed to do – in this case, building our confidence level.

Below, you'll see the areas where you might feel pain and find the year where trauma may have occurred that impacted your confidence.

The Seven Major Chakras

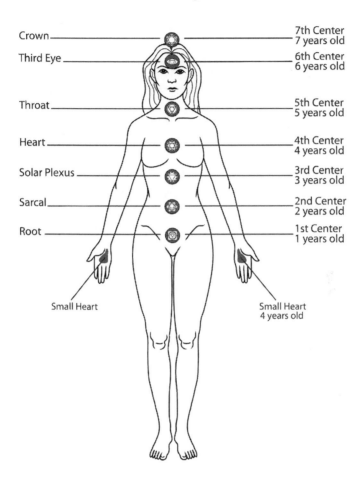

Crown — 7th Center / 7 years old

Third Eye — 6th Center / 6 years old

Throat — 5th Center / 5 years old

Heart — 4th Center / 4 years old

Solar Plexus — 3rd Center / 3 years old

Sarcal — 2nd Center / 2 years old

Root — 1st Center / 1 years old

Small Heart

Small Heart 4 years old

First, think of an action you would like to take but don't feel confident enough to do. Next, close your eyes and notice where in your body you feel discomfort. Use the picture above to locate the year. Now that you know the age ranges, sit quietly and ask yourself what happened that year that really upset you. Your initial inclination might be to say, "I don't know," or "I don't remember." Please, don't let yourself off the hook so fast. Ask your subconscious over and over. Don't dismiss your thoughts too quickly. Stay with the inquiry for a while and take a guess by completing the end of this sentence:

I know I don't know what happened,
but if I knew, it would have been _____.

One of my clients, Lindsey, was going to interview for a job promotion. She was a successful manager with an excellent performance record, but she hadn't interviewed for a job in eight years. Lindsey had great charisma but needed to improve her A-game since high-level executives would interview her. She was nervous. Lindsey quickly learned some of the techniques for a great interview during our preparation and memorized the key points.

At the end of the interview, she called and shared that she was too nervous and thought she did okay, but not great. A few days later, Lindsey learned that she didn't get the job. A week later, she got feedback from her boss that she did terribly in the interview. Lindsey didn't answer their questions; she mumbled information that she memorized that had nothing to do with their questions. The interviewers noticed that she was too nervous and got her some water. They took a bit of a break because they knew her business results, but it didn't help. Lindsey's fear drove her to defeat.

I got to work with her again for another interview for a similar position. This time, I decided to put the business books aside and work with her energy centers to find the root of the problem.

When I asked Lindsey what happened in her childhood that made her afraid of failure, she didn't know. I asked about her parents and what type of upbringing she experienced. She immediately defended her parents and shared how great they were, even though they were strict. I asked her to close her eyes and think about the interview. Then, I asked her to notice where in her body she felt the anxiety. She told me the discomfort was in her gut. This area is the solar plexus, responsible for our confidence, willpower, and self-trust.

Once I knew that it was a confidence-level problem, I narrowed down a range of events for Lindsey. She was afraid of failure. When she was three, ten, or seventeen years old, something made her terrified of failure. When we feel fear, our body goes into stress mode. We don't think straight and miss opportunities. Our biological systems prepare us for fight or flight. We lose connection with our higher purpose because our body believes it needs to survive.

I pressured Lindsey again to dig into her past and find a time when something happened that upset her more than usual. She couldn't think of anything at first, but then she remembered an event when she was about ten years old. She played soccer with a team. The league was going to travel, and the players had to try out. She felt she was a good player and as good as most girls, but she didn't make the team. All of her closest friends got selected but her. At that time, she began to cry as she remembered how she felt. She didn't want to cry because she thought it was silly to cry about something that had happened more than twenty-four years ago. But she was devastated for weeks after losing her position on the team. Lindsey felt she also lost her closest friends because they spent more time with the other players on the team. Her parents didn't make a big deal of it, but she remembered her mother was disappointed.

Lindsey continued to play soccer, but she became terrified of failing. Her ten-year-old child made decisions that didn't support a thirty-four-year-old woman today. Yet, unconsciously, every time something is at stake, she bucks the current because her mind triggers those fears and processes them as a ten-year-old rather than a mature, successful woman.

I asked Lindsey to have a conversation with her young self and have compassion for her. Unfortunately, she didn't make the team. Yet, people who don't make the team can learn resilience, connection, and positive self-talk. Not making the team was not the end of the world. It was hard, but it didn't have to damage her self-worth. Ten-year-olds don't have the maturity to process loss, self-worth, and positive self-talk without help.

The conclusion Lindsey arrived at as a child didn't serve her. Every test or competition she encountered was treated as a potential for emotional and physical devastation. It eroded her confidence for years. As a result, she worked harder than most people, kept her hand in everything, and constantly went above and beyond. But these were old ways of being. We don't have to deplete our energy to get what we want. We just need a bit more confidence.

No one could blame Lindsey. She didn't have good role models. Many of our female ancestors who had some confidence paid a high price for showing it off. They were shamed, discriminated against, harassed out of the tribal mindset, and even killed. Over time, women with confidence were conditioned to believe that having it would lead to too many risks. Their voices were often silenced by the social norms of the time. So it's not a surprise that if you believe you don't have a good level of confidence, your mind is doing what it does best to protect you. It built a few walls around your confidence, so if you don't feel it, that's why. But you can change that today.

Confidence and Willpower

Some people mistake confidence with willpower. Confidence is a power, but willpower is an action led by pure determination. People who need confidence but don't have the proper foundation will resort to their willpower. Having willpower is important; however, as it lives in the perimeter of our Power of Confidence, it can be used as a propeller to initiate a desired outcome. But willpower alone isn't enough. We can't sustain it over a long period of time. You need self-trust, which is confidence.

When we try to lose weight and begin with a rigid diet, we resort to our willpower, which is very strong in some people. We will muscle our way through sixty-six days (the time to create a new habit), but the strict regime can crumble at any time when we experience an emotional setback or a big distraction. So willpower isn't a long-term strategy. It was never meant to be. So how do we use our confidence instead of betting against ourselves with willpower?

A more nurturing way of having and building confidence is through developing self-trust. Pause now. Take three deep and slow breaths.

Breathe in, hold it, and breathe out.
Breathe in, hold it, and breathe out.
Breathe in, hold it, and breathe out.

The three breaths signal your body to relax and open yourself to experience the energy of the words below. Now, read the two words, and feel the feeling associated with them. Close your eyes and tap into the emotions of the two words.

Willpower - Self-Trust

The word *willpower* has more demanding energy than the word *self-trust*. The word *willpower* is very masculine, yang energy. On the contrary, the word *self-trust* has grounding energy. It's feminine and yin energy.

The world has been operating with willpower energy, and that's why we have been conditioned to work under pressure for centuries. Women have witnessed it in men who use it to display what looks like confidence. But willpower has been responsible for stress, burnout, depletion, exhaustion, adrenal fatigue, and other diseases in women and men.

Now, it's time for the energy of self-trust to take the stage. Having confidence with self-trust will take you from a firm grip to inner peace. Because we live in a place of duality, we may need a bit of willpower to start and then operate in the self-trust arena. Again, remember the yin-yang symbol.

The ability to trust ourselves feels peaceful, grounding, quiet, encompassing, and fulfilling. Having self-trust as a foundation for your Power of Confidence is like feeling the water pounding against the wall with infinite patience, knowing that it has to go through and carve a new path, just as it built canyons.

Again, your confidence is inside of you, although it's well-guarded. You can access it at a moment's notice. Just like you can recall a sad event and cry, confidence can be recalled and awakened from inside of you. If you did the exercise above, you got glimpses of your confidence, even if you still experienced it through your willpower.

Bring Out Confidence

Confidence is the life power that allows you to show up in your true colors to the world. Unfortunately, your old beliefs about your ability to be confident, either true or not, will support or sabotage you in times of need and growth. All growth requires risk, and if you don't muster the confidence to take a chance, you limit your potential.

Three-year-old children who grew up in safe environments have a good level of confidence. We have seen them growing older, often jumping in the pool without knowing how to swim, taking the toys away from other older children, spitting out food they don't want to eat, talking to strangers, and venturing out in the supermarket and toy stores without hesitation. Likewise, when three-year-old girls are loved, encouraged, nurtured, and free to express themselves, they tend to grow up with the awareness they can be, have, and do anything they desire. That's confidence in its pure form.

When the environment is disempowering to girls, where they are told to be silent, not to talk to adults, and often criticized, they hush their power of confidence once they become women. Over time, they forget that they ever had it.

Many cultures tend to assign confidence traits to boys. Not only do we see it in cartoons while growing up, but we see it on the playground. Adventurous girls are called "tomboys," which isn't usually considered a compliment. As an adult, often in the presence of men, women with no confidence withdraw and hold back their opinions. They remove their names from the race to promotion and expect men to win. When the opportunity falls in their laps, they pass because they don't know how to walk in confident shoes.

Confidence Measurer

Generally, confidence just isn't a trait nurtured in women. Our confident female role models were called the "B" word. Men tend to see confidence in women as a barrier to their own success. Unfortunately, women even put down other women who display confidence. Women are also called "too bossy" when they show their confidence. So, where is the balance?

Each situation calls for a different level of confidence. The problem isn't the amount of confidence but what people perceive to be the appropriate level. We have a big problem here. People believe women need more confidence, but no one can agree on what "appropriate" means. Oddly, we never seem to have this conversation about men's confidence level.

To begin, we need to have an honest conversation about it. We must appreciate the women with high confidence levels as much as we value those levels in men. Some people mistake confidence for arrogance, and no one likes an arrogant woman or man. Confidence, on the other hand, is simply the ability to believe in themselves. In women, that's a level of self-trust. Confident people trust themselves, and their behavior is congruent with their confidence. Arrogance is about trying to position themselves above others. Arrogant people are egotists and show themselves off by putting other people down.

We can see confidence in how people dress, walk, talk, and be-have, and we believe it comes from outside of them. But confidence is an inside job. Do you have the traits of a confident woman? Read the following section to discover.

The Five Levels of Confidence

I've learned that confidence is built on mindset and preparation. For example, if I'm running a marathon, I need to prepare my body for physical exertion and my mind to believe I can accomplish the running. Over the years, I've found that there are five levels of confidence:

Level One – People in level one have zero percentage of self-trust and zero percentage of preparation. They tend to act like they have too much confidence. You can spot them by the constant state of discontent. They don't want to risk the status quo or get prepared, so they don't do anything. Instead, they play it down. They say things like, "I'd go for that promotion, but I don't want that much respon-sibility," or "I'd rather be single than meet those creepy guys online."

Level Two – People in level two have one hundred percent self-trust and zero preparation. They are the wingers of the world. They have no foundation for the amount of confidence they display. They need to do a presentation but don't prepare for it. Instead, they show up and wing it. Sometimes, they do well, and other times, not so much. Their excessive winging is false confidence, and often they use a massive amount of willpower to get what they want. Don't get me wrong – winging isn't always bad. It just may not get you where you want to go because you can't leave everything to fate and willpower when you lack preparation.

Level Three – People in level three have zero self-trust and one hundred percent preparation. They prepare so much that they don't ever take any action. They feel they aren't ready. Many writers, painters, and musicians are in level three. They work five, ten, or even fifteen years on a project they feel is never good enough. They believe their work is too short, too long, too amateur, too simple, too complex, etc., and they never grow from their level of insecurity.

Level Four – People in level four have about fifty percent self-trust and fifty percent preparation. Their level of self-reliability and preparation are balanced, and action is usually taken (or not taken) based on their emotional state. People in level four are like the middle child. They don't want the spotlight from the top or the bottom. They like the middle and don't commit to one side or the other unless pushed or challenged, usually through willpower. They tend to set their expectations low and surpass them so they're happy. There is merit in this level, but they tend not to grow to their full potential.

Level Five – People in level five have about seventy-five percent self-trust and seventy-five percent preparation. The math is not wrong. Hear me out. That's where you find the most successful people regardless of your definition of success. These level five people work on the edge of their tiptoes. They always work just above their capacity. They go for a promotion that they're almost qualified for, ask for the raise before looking for a better paying job, and are willing to know, do, and have what it takes to go to the next level. Then, they make a move just before they find themselves fully ready.

People may call them lucky or overnight success, but there's no luck in mindset or preparation. Frida Kahlo didn't become famous for her first painting. Toni Morrison took seven years after her first book and many books after that before her writing was recognized. Billie Holiday was singing in many nightclubs for years before she was offered a record deal. Having enough self-trust and preparation or practice seems to be the key to having the confidence to stick our neck out and get what we want in life.

Regardless of your confidence level right now, it can be changed when you're willing to do the work. Preparation helps your mindset, and your mindset helps you prepare.

Support for Confidence Powers

What level are you? Are you in level one, two, three, four, or five? If you don't know the next step for you, confidence may not be on your radar yet, which means you are at the base level. You could try learning a new hobby to activate your Power of Confidence. Perhaps you want to travel the world, learn to play the piano, change jobs, or call an ex-boyfriend you often think about. Having a meaningful cause will inspire your confidence level to move beyond the status quo. We need you and your confidence.

The following questions will shine a light on your mindset level and confidence. Take three deep breaths, and answer the questions honestly:

1) Do I feel confident?
2) Do I take risks?
3) Do I trust myself?
4) Do I display confidence at work?
5) Do I display confidence in my relationships?
6) Do I tend to go after what I want?
7) Do I stick to my gut feelings?
8) Would I go on a blind date?
9) Do I rely on my willpower to go for what I want?
10) Do I prepare for what I want to achieve?

If you answered yes to eight or more questions, congratulations! You're doing great with your Confidence Power.

If you answered yes to five or more questions, you need to energize your confidence power.

If you answered yes to four or fewer questions, you need to rebuild your confidence power.

Write the insights you received in your journal or book companion.

Body, Mind & Wisdom School:
How Do You Get to Confidence Level Five?

Here are four suggestions to improve your level of confidence.

One – Mind Your Mindset

Remember that every woman has a level of confidence waiting to be expressed even though no one is one hundred percent confident one hundred percent of the time. So, you need to know where you are and bring your subconscious mind to light.

Your confidence level was influenced by your environment in childhood, but it isn't a death sentence. Before you start blaming your parents and every adult in your childhood, you need to learn that your subconscious made decisions about your confidence that still impacts you today. Those decisions were meant to keep you safe and honor a level of self-esteem you felt was adequate.

Answer these questions to discover some more insights about you and your level of confidence:

1) Do you tend to over-prepare or wing?
2) What do you believe about your confidence?
3) Are you stuck in your comfort zone?
4) When was the last time you used your confidence to get out of your comfort zone?
5) Was confidence encouraged or discouraged in your home growing up?
6) Can you identify any woman with a good level of confidence in your circle? Do you like or dislike her?
7) If you had high confidence levels, what would you use it for?

Now that you're aware of some of your beliefs, you can change them by increasing your level of self-trust. First, you must change the unsupportive thoughts you have about confidence. How do you really feel about confident people? If they are negative, change them now. You can start with affirmations. For example, write this affirmation with lipstick on your mirror or shower: "I Trust Myself." The repetition of this affirmation will work as well as the initial willpower, but with less pressure.

Be willing to walk on your tiptoes for a while. If you have an impulse, read your affirmation and go for it. It's okay to start slow and get better with time than to not take any step. Again, you can use a little willpower, but only to take the first step. For example, you could use it to set up your exercise clothes the night before going to the gym, buying fruits and vegetables on Sundays, or watching job interview classes before posting your resumes. You don't want to rely on masculine willpower for too long, which was meant to sabotage you. I repeat, willpower is not a long-term strategy. If you feel you're too comfortable in your old ways, it's time to change it.

Two – Be Willing to Risk

The Power of Confidence can't be exercised unless something is at stake. It will surface or hide when you risk your reputation, a job, a promotion, relationships, etc.

It's easy for people to feel confident when alone within the safety of their four-bedroom walls watching television. You don't risk anything when you binge-watch Netflix; there's nothing to gain or lose. But that's comfort, not confidence. True confidence comes when you step outside of your comfort zone. This is the time when you make a decision to go after something you've wanted for some time but have been afraid to risk your status quo.

I've learned over the years that true dreams don't die. Perhaps you've been thinking for years of opening a store, going back to school, asking for a promotion, or whatever goal you dreamed of. Do it! Our destiny will always call us to it over and over. And if after a while it doesn't happen for you, celebrate! Know that the universe is set up to make you a winner, so there is a better door for you. Now that you know that, you are a bit more ready for other higher risks.

Another suggestion: open your closet and select an outfit that exudes confidence. Get dressed and walk with confidence in front of the mirror. Stand tall, shoulders back, and feel the confidence in your gut. The color yellow and sunshine will energize the solar plexus chakra center. Remember, confidence is an emotion!

Then, talk with confidence in the mirror. Practice confidence often. Your mind will remember how confident you can become.

Three – Exercise Confidence

Confidence is also a muscle; if you don't exercise it, its power diminishes. It also has memory. In a short time, it can awaken from its dormant stage.

You can exercise your confidence by signing up for a class, volunteering for a new charity, going out to dinner alone, traveling alone, asking to be featured in a magazine or show, applying for a new job that you're *almost* qualified for, or asking for a promotion.

People tend to be more confident when they have a partner, so consider this book your spiritual partner. We, all of the readers, are with you in spirit. When you show your confidence, you help everyone. Know that other women who display their confidence are helping you, too. Also, share your confidence in social media. You will be amazed how many women will celebrate you.

But if you haven't shown your confidence before, don't expect to have confidence without dancing with it. Be willing to get a bit messy. It will all be worth it.

Try the exercise I did with Lindsey. First, find the emotional trauma in your third, tenth, or seventeenth years. Then, process it as an adult. Talk to your inner child about it, feel empathy for her, and don't dismiss her feelings. Instead, have compassion for her. Let your tears heal her and you. If you find yourself feeling too angry about your past trauma, please go back and read chapter one: "The Power of Nurturing." This isn't a time for blame. You will heal and open your powers one at a time.

One more thing: send thoughts of encouragement to all women struggling with their confidence today during your meditation or prayer. We could all use some spiritual help on this.

Four – Become Your Ally

To build confidence, you must become your own ally. You can do that by no longer predicting your failures. Instead, expect to win. If you think you'll fail, you'll fail. No level of confidence in the world will buck that. Your subconscious will influence your actions to confirm that you can't venture safely out of your comfort zone.

You already know that to have confidence, you need to prepare and have the right mindset. No one is ever one hundred percent ready, so you must leap.

Let's do a quick exercise. Think of something you want. Perhaps it's a new job, more money, a great relationship, or a new home. Pick one thing and evoke the feeling of hope that you could get it. Just hope for it and notice how you feel.

Now, let go of the hope. Think about the same thing you hoped for. Instead of hoping, expect that you will get it. Feel the excitement of getting it. Imagine what it would feel like when you actually get it. See the vision and feel that you have achieved this dream.

Do you feel the difference? From this day on, there is no more hope—only the *expectation of success*. This simple exercise will build your confidence levels because you're investing in your success instead of possible failures.

Calling Your Confidence Forward

In 1977, a sixty-three-year-old grandmother rescued her grandson from under a parked car. She lifted the Buick with one hand and pulled the child to safety with the other. Did she need her confidence to lift the car? You'd better believe it. If anyone had asked her if she could lift a Buick that weighed about three and a half thousand pounds before the incident, she would undoubtedly have denied it. But the confidence was inside of her all along, and her emotions pulled it out. Again, confidence is inside of you.

I began to write in my teenage years, solely in Portuguese. I had great ideas and a poet's mind. Starting in 1996, I wrote many chapters of an untitled book about women in business that never got past an outline and chapter four. Being Brazilian, English isn't my first language, and in college, my first English professor discouraged my writing. I lost my confidence.

In 2014, after an emotional incident, I began to get more serious about writing. I worked with my confidence and published my first book, *Women, Rice and Beans,* in 2016. About four months before the issue date, my level of confidence was non-existent. I had a publishing to-do list that was two pages long, and I was paralyzed with fear. Three weeks went by, and I was unable to complete anything on that list.

I was afraid of failing, being criticized, and even losing my job. My mind paralyzed me because it was protecting me from the failure, disappointment, and unemployment I perceived would come with the book. I finally called my coach, and she helped me reset my mindset.

Remember when I said that confidence can only be exercised when you have something at stake? In this case, it was my life purpose. True confidence won't show up because your buddy dared you to do something silly like jumping into a freezing lake. Confidence shows up when it really matters. Once I had made peace with the worst-case scenarios, confidence silenced my fears.

Where to Use Confidence

The Power of Confidence can be used in all areas of your life:

Career: Asking for a job, asking for a raise, changing careers.

Health: Facing a diagnosis, deciding on treatment.

Finance: Facing/negotiating debt, selling a home, asking for help.

Relationships: Ending a relationship, asking for what you want, breaking ties with negative people, asking for help.

Education:	Changing careers, learning a new skill, going back to school.
Creativity:	Exposing your work, selling your work, asking for feedback.
Family:	Forgiving a family member, exposing a family secret, setting boundaries.

List one to three areas of your life that could be infused with a good dose of confidence:

1. _____

2. _____

3. _____

Women who practice the Power of Confidence are like precious little diamonds we see shining if we observe them from space. Their light travels far. Women with confidence can be spotted in their community because they found a home, cause, job, or people who not only need them but who crave their ways of being. If you are a woman with confidence or are on your way there, you must shine and own your light. Walk your brightness like you were invited to the parade. Stay in your power by knowing that you know. You are opening space for other diamonds to come behind you. There is power in quiet confidence. When you are congruent, you are being guided.

P.S. One more thing: you will need to use your confidence when you begin to work with the Power of Intuition in chapter six. Be ready to magnify your light.

Chapter 4

The Power of Compassion

"If your compassion does not include yourself,
it is incomplete."

— BUDDHA

The fourth power every woman has is the Power of Compassion. It's expressed from our heart center located in the middle of our chest. This chakra center is influenced by the colors green and pink and the element of air. There are also two small heart chakras located in the palm of our hands, which you will learn more about in the later chapters. This power is responsible for our ability to become centered in our connection with ourselves, other people, and experiences through our feelings. This energy is also called love. When it's magnified, we embody it as compassion.

The word compassion literally means "to suffer together." This power reminds us that we all are *one*. Compassion is the highest emotion a person can feel, and according to spiritual teacher David Hawkins, it has the highest frequency. Compassion compels us to relieve other people's suffering even if we don't have a direct relationship with them.

When we look at the usefulness of compassion, it seems that God played a trick on humanity because genuine compassion can only be expressed once we experience the discomfort of sharing someone else's pain, which most people want to avoid. Yet, the power of compassion allows us to be in the highest state of our humanity. When we share the pain of others, we become *one*. This experience is what the greatest masters of our history prophesized.

There are millions of ways to exercise compassion. Like the water, food, and shelter we need to live, compassion is necessary to make us more human. Practicing it doesn't require much. We just need to feel it. We don't need to find a cause, other people, or animals to feel it. There's no need to go on the internet, research the worst world crises, and make a donation either. Although that's how some people choose to demonstrate and feel compassion, there are other ways closer to home.

Another usefulness of the Power of Compassion is how it opens humanity to higher experiences. You could be in a penthouse in New York City and be one with the people of Nepal on the other side of the planet by feeling their suffering. It's good for compassion to linger and stretch in our lives. Being in a state of compassion strengthens your heart and opens you up to the intelligence available in your heart center.

There are millions of synapse connections in the heart that are similar to the ones in the brain. We have also learned that the heart, like the brain, has memory. Science has just confirmed what ancient spiritual people knew over centuries ago – that the heart is extremely powerful, and this is big news!

There are two well-documented cases showing that the heart remembers. First, after receiving a heart transplant, a patient began to crave the foods the heart donor used to love and do things the donor used to do, which the receiver never did before. The second case showed a young girl who received a heart from another child who was murdered. The child who received the heart began to recall the events of the little girl's murder and led the police to arrest the perpetrator.

Understanding the power of our heart means that we are no longer victims of a mindset that wants to protect us and make decisions that may not be aligned with our higher purpose. Instead, we can connect with our "heartset" that wants to build bridges of love, healing, compassion, and generosity, making decisions that are aligned with our purpose and the agreements we've made to help humanity move forward.

But genuine compassion starts within. Self-compassion is the primary function of the Power of Compassion. Take three deep breaths right now before you read the following sentence so that you can see, hear, and feel your inner being calling for your practice of self-compassion. Breathe in and breathe out. Then, do it again, and on the third breath, hold it for ten seconds before releasing it.

You must love, forgive, and accept yourself and all that comes from you before feeling compassion for others.

Read the above sentence again and again until it sinks in. Please don't be quick to dismiss its meaning. This is important. When on a plane, we have heard from the flight attendants that if the cabinet pressure drops, put your oxygen mask on first before helping others, even if the others are your children or elderly parents. You can't give to others from a state of depletion. You can't show compassion to your neighbor until you feel it for yourself.

Training to Be Loved

A practice of self-compassion calls for us to fully love ourselves with all our faults. That requires a tremendous amount of self-awareness because we don't always catch when we become unkind to ourselves. Sometimes, our self-abuse is well-disguised in the way we work, eat, drink, rest, or enjoy life. We become accustomed to self-abuse, and after a while, it becomes the norm. Often, we're quick to recognize that behavior in others, but not in ourselves. There's a good chance that if you grew up being scolded, abused, criticized, and spanked, you may have a different understanding of what love and compassion are because that's how you learned to experience love.

We learn how to treat ourselves from the way we were treated by adults when we were young. If you had compassionate parents, you are likely to know how to treat yourself well. If you didn't, your level of self-compassion might be compromised. We can always spot someone struggling with the Power of Compassion when they have trouble relating to others, especially romantically.

Many people who struggle with self-compassion tend to believe that they fell in love with the wrong person or they're unlucky. They find themselves with partners who don't accept them, don't meet their expectations, or are without partners and friends altogether. They feel they can't find anyone to love them right. But that seems to be another trick on humanity. If you believe you've attracted the wrong partners or can't find anyone at all, that is just your life mirroring your level of self-love. If you feel you aren't loved, you probably haven't loved yourself the way you want to be loved. I know this is hard to hear. But before you dismiss this ancient wisdom as I too have done before, I beg you to continue to be open and listen to it with your heart.

The lives of women through the ages didn't leave room for them to learn love and self-acceptance at their core. For centuries, women were conditioned to be "good girls" and believed they needed to marry to be even half-valued. In the thirteenth century, the average age of a married woman was seventeen to twenty-two. Some women of status would get married as early as nine years old through an arranged marriage to a twenty-year-old or older groom. In the sixteenth century, the median age of brides was twenty-two. In the eighteenth century, the average age of brides increased to twenty-six years old. Not too long ago, women expected to be married before the age of thirty. At thirty-one years old, women were considered "old maids." There was also an economic fact at play. A daughter was thought to be an expense for families. The parents had to pay the groom to marry their daughters as if they were a piece of junk to be removed from the home. If the family didn't have means, the daughter had little chance to find a suitable husband. In that case, the young daughter was often matched to a much older man, sometimes forty years her senior, or sent to a convent.

In many cultures, the birth of a daughter wasn't celebrated like the birth of a son. It was a time of mourning rather than joy. Getting rid of daughters through early marriage was an economic and social decision. Many families didn't put up a fight when their daughter wanted to marry young. Having an unmarried girl pregnant in the home brought shame to the child and the family, and it happened often.

For many years, young pregnant girls were sent away to have their babies and "pay for their sins" with hard work and humiliation. Even when abortion became legal and women aborted a child, the shame they faced didn't go away after they got married.

For centuries, women were forced to settle for partners they didn't want to meet society's unrealistic expectations. Women were trained to be wives and put their husband's needs above their own. As a result, women without means were prepared to be good wives. Training began when they were young.

When I was nine years old, I was taught how to cook, clean, and take care of the house, even though we had a housekeeper. I would often hear, "Good job. You can get married now," when I cooked a great dish. Although more women choose to marry later in life these days, and some choose to not marry at all, we still find girls role-playing their wedding with Barbie and Ken dolls.

Of course, whether or not a woman chooses to marry, people weren't meant to be completely alone. Formal marriage was established by the church to hold men responsible for supporting women they impregnated and the resulting children. Many people didn't get married in churches. In the past, a marriage ceremony could happen in a home, bar, or just outside the church front door, as long as the bride and groom said, "I do." Also, in some cultures, people would be considered married if they had sex.

These days, most women are free to marry or not, although arranged marriages are still a practice in some places. They are also free to love, but they are *not* free to "not love." You may think that you have the right to not love anybody, but loving others is your admission ticket to life.

To love is the essence of a woman. Our heart center is charged to love, and when the love is full, we experience compassion more readily. Not loving would mean we aren't fully living. Since we can't live without love, it would be a good idea to begin working with love, first, by discarding the concepts of false love, understanding the difference between romance and real love, and then commencing to love ourselves. That's when self-compassion will come out and play.

We all love ourselves at our core, even though some of you may not be aware of it. You may not feel what that love looks like because you compare your life with the love you see in romantic movies. *Gone with the Wind, Casablanca, An Affair to Remember, Pride and Prejudice, The Notebook,* and other films did an amazing job of personifying romantic love that touched us deeply. Most of us wish to be loved the way Clark Gable's character Rhett Butler or Humphrey Bogart's character Rick Blaine love their protagonists. Romance novels are the most popular genre of books sold. This is an indication that women are craving love. But these movies, books, and TV shows are only good for inspiring you to love. Real love requires your heart to be open. I'm not asking you to stop indulging in the romances you read and watch, but I *am* asking you to know the difference between real love and romance.

The truth is if you want the kind of love old enough to transcend time with ease, you need to start loving yourself and practicing self-compassion. Most of us no longer have the social pressure to be married or have children. It's now your choice. However, you may have been conditioned not to love yourself because of how love was expressed in your home. Many people have become tired of disappointments and given up on love. If so, please reconsider.

Women and Dogs

The other day, I took a walk in the park. It was still winter, and I sat on one of the benches in the sun. Nearby, I saw two people training dogs. They held long orange leashes but gave the dogs little room to run. They would tell the dogs to sit or obey some command, and the dogs received a treat when they did. During my time in the sun, the dogs received many treats. As I walked home, I began to connect this type of domestication of animals to women. Since they were young, women are domesticated to behave in a certain way in order to get a treat. The treat is approval or love. Take your pick. They are taught how to sit, eat, comb their hair, dress, speak, hide their sensuality, and have proper feminine traits that are well received in society.

I began wondering what happened to women when they don't follow the family's domestication plan. Are they denied love and approval? Does the technique they use with dogs work for women? Do women understand who is in charge when they are deprived of their freedom? And mostly, would women still love the trainers unconditionally as dogs do after being starved of freedom?

I remember my dog Ruffos, a puppy my boyfriend gave me when I was eighteen years old. I took him to my parents' house because I couldn't keep a dog in my apartment. Ruffos was a gorgeous dog with light orange-brown fur and beautiful blueish eyes. It was what Brazilians call a "viralata," which translates to "turn-cans," or a mutt. Ruffos was abandoned as a puppy when my boyfriend found him on the street.

In Brazil at that time, dogs were purchased to protect houses against robbery. My family already had two German Shepherds trained to protect the home overnight. Mutts were adopted for the same reason but with less status. The dogs slept during the day and were let free in the yard at night to guard the house. Ruffos and the other two dogs got along well. He had a great spirit and liked to run free. He used to jump the fence around the house, scaring people who walked on the sidewalk too close to the house, but he was a friendly dog and never bit anyone.

In the mornings, when my brother would let the dogs in, Ruffos usually wasn't around. He would leave in the night, run free and wild, and return home late in the mornings. My brother would call out his name from both sides of the sidewalk (my parents lived in a corner house), and Ruffos would show up eventually to get a beating from my brother. That's how they trained dogs back then. But, after many free nights and smacking mornings, Ruffos didn't come back one day. I found out about a month later when I visited.

That winter day, as I walked the long way home, I questioned if some women could be domesticated for love. When women no longer need men for survival but are still trained to behave a certain way in exchange for love, attention, and approval, can they remember who they are after years of "good girl" conditioning? How many women would rebel, leave, and never return like my dog?

By the end of that day, I realized that I was trained to be a good girl. When I was growing up, my free spirit would forget the domestication and follow the wind, and when I returned, there were no treats. For many years, I acted like a good girl, as many women have, in order to be accepted and loved.

I left my parents' house around my eighteenth birthday just like Ruffos did – I didn't come home one day. I had no plan, but I didn't want to receive the punishment. A few days later I returned to get my clothes and didn't come back. One would think that I learned to be undomesticated at that point, but I didn't. It takes lots of self-love to heal generations of expectations.

Would Anyone Love Me If They Knew Who I Really Was?

Being a good girl is exhausting. Wanting to behave as a bad girl feels physically draining. After years of conditioning, women may be at the fork in the road and not know which way to go. Their training will tell them to go right, and their anger will pull to the left. After being at the crossroads, my advice is, "It's best to stay put for a while to find out how you love." Because the way you love is the way you *are* loved. If you love with conditions, that's the way you'll be loved.

Do you still respond to the manipulation of your upbringing? Is love withheld because of the way you behave? How do you love others? How do you share your essence with yourself and others? Self-love is more than a bubble bath or a weekly massage.

Self-care, for the most part, is self-love. The way you accept your body, mind, and spirit's nature is the higher path to the Power of

Compassion. I invite you to ponder these questions above and learn how you love.

Your Nurturing Powers already know how to heal your wounds. You just need a little time, a little space, and a considerable dose of self-love as you bathe in the river of kindness available *for* you *from* you.

Love wasn't meant to be a bargaining power. In his book, *Love-ability,* Dr. Robert Holden shares his views on love. He believes that we weren't meant to give or receive love, or even be love, but to *know* love. I think this is a lovely way to exercise our powers.

The Power of Compassion leads us to know love recklessly by throwing all caution to the wind. We can't know love if we don't love ourselves first. We must clean the muck from our perceptions about love. The muck is all the conditioning we were exposed to in the name of love. But it wasn't *love.*

As you pause and begin to know love and feel self-love to access your Power of Compassion, you will be called to remember your original love and how you used to love before the domestication. Because the conditioning has an imprint in your DNA, your healing will call on you to heal both your ancestors and your offspring. This is a powerful moment in your lineage. Don't take it lightly.

To reconnect with your self-love, I suggest that you get up in the morning and find a quiet place where you won't be disturbed. Close your eyes, take three deep breaths, and call in your soul. You don't have to know how; just ask your soul to express the love it feels for you. Stay there and hold that intention. Keep asking over and over until you feel infinite self-love. This is one of the most beautiful experiences you will have in this physical world. It may take a few tries, but it will happen. Knowing and feeling the love of your soul is life-changing.

You can do this practice at any time, but it will be easier in the morning. And when you do, your perception of love will expand. Your knowing of love will heal your life. Do this practice daily if you feel called to heal your heart center.

At this point in your journey to high states of compassion, it won't matter what you did or didn't do or what conditions and limitations you've learned in the past. Unlimited self-love is powerful medicine. Once you love yourself, you're open to receiving love.

One thing people misunderstand about love is that it's always available to everyone. If you don't experience love, it isn't because people don't love you, but because you don't love yourself. You can't experience what isn't in your awareness. If you don't know love intimately, it will be challenging for you to experience it.

But please don't beat yourself up if this is challenging for you. Depending on your conclusions about love, it could hit you in the head, and you wouldn't recognize it even if everyone told you what it was. In time, however, you'll be able to open yourself to it because every single one of us *is* love.

To Trust or Not to Trust

One day, I was talking to a friend who had left her previous job and didn't know what to do with the few thousand dollars she had in a retirement account. She didn't make much money. I explained her options and suggested that she could roll it into a retirement fund. I also told her if she had credit card debt, she could use some of the money to pay that down. She looked disappointed with my response. Then, I asked her what she wanted to do with the money. She said she wanted to take a trip to Israel.

I explained to her the tax consequences and some of the rules of money. She was approaching fifty years old and didn't have a retirement fund. But my advice was based on my truth. So I told her to tap into her heart, and then she would know what to do with the money.

She replied to me that she couldn't trust her heart because the heart always deceives us. I was surprised by her comment, to which she said, "It's in the Bible." I didn't try to convince her what I knew about the heart. Instead, I let her decide what to do with the money without any argument from me.

Afterwards, I did a little digging. First, I found in the Bible: "Let not your hearts be troubled. Believe in God; believe also in me [Jesus]" (John 14:1). Then, I found, "The heart is more deceitful than all else and is desperately sick, who can understand it?" (Jeremiah 17:9).

First, scholars have found too many mistranslations in the hundreds of versions of the Bible in English alone. Second, far too many texts were omitted from the Bible over the past seven hundred years with the intent to keep Christians in the dark and stop them from questioning what Jesus really meant. That way, people would follow what the Church wanted them to believe. Third, if the text is correctly translated and not added later, then John and Jeremiah were two left-brained individuals who didn't know that Jesus *is* love, and *love* exists in everyone. Therefore, the spirit of Jesus lives within everyone. If you believe in love or Jesus or God, then you can trust your heart.

But some people simply won't trust their hearts. Instead, they believe a piece of paper written thousands of years ago, which was translated, misinterpreted, and changed over the years to suit who was in charge. Moreover, they aren't allowed to interpret what was written in the Bible. So who knows what the author really meant?

When you work with the Power of Compassion, you understand that hearts are opinionated, but they don't boss you around – minds do. Hearts have an opinion about everything and will only guide you if you ask. To access that guidance, you need to be in a heart-coherence state. When you're desperate, overwhelmed, or angry, the directions you hear aren't coming from your heart. That's from your mind, which wants to rush you out of the trouble into safety as they perceived based on past experience.

Through slow breathing, you will reach a heart-coherent state that will show you that you already are in a safe space. Then, you can access guidance. This practice of finding congruence through your heart connection is often achieved when you meditate.

I never asked my friend what she did with the money, nor did I try to convince her that we could trust our hearts. I just hope she followed her heart because it knows better when it's harmonized with the highest part of us.

Can I Forgive Myself?

When you discover self-love, you'll experience it as potent energy taking over multiple areas of your life. If you were not taught to love yourself with the same kindness you extend to others, that will be a significant shift. The Power of Compassion will begin to express itself in your life, and you will find yourself less critical and judgmental, first of yourself and then of others.

There is no reason to penalize yourself for mistakes. You may have learned the concept of constant punishment because of your early domestication, but that isn't true. We don't have to become inferior beings and take an eye for an eye, as "written" in the Bible, which was mistranslated and manually adjusted by a few people to control the masses. Women have suffered enough, and they already have punished themselves enough just for being female. Of course, we can get angry, curse, cry, and not hide our feelings as we were taught to do, but mostly, we need to love ourselves enough to stop carrying those heavy burdens that feel like large boulders on our backs.

It's easier to extend forgiveness to others, but we must do the same for ourselves. Unfortunately, many women may not be consciously aware that they need to forgive themselves. We have the habit of hiding our mistakes in the back of our minds because we learned that mistakes must be punished just like we were conditioned in childhood. But we need to become aware of this need to forgive ourselves and then do something about it.

When we look at history, we find examples of severe punishments to teach humanity the difference between right and wrong. They were not commands from a higher power; they were dictated by men. The main problem is that what was wrong fifty years ago is entirely acceptable today, and what was acceptable a hundred years ago is against the law. For example, slavery, drinking alcohol, using drugs, marrying a child, etc. So how do we reconcile these?

The Power of Compassion calls for us to fully forgive ourselves before we can forgive others. I mean everything: stealing, cheating, betraying, and even killing. Forgiveness isn't lip service, nor does it let us off the hook and enable us to continue to hurt others.

Not too long ago, forgiveness could be purchased with money. Depending on your donation to the church or how much money you left in your will for them, you could secure your salvation and avoid going to hell. Still today, in the Catholic Church, forgiveness is given by God through the act of confession with a priest. In this model, you could hurt someone every Monday and be forgiven on Sundays before Mass.

In my view, the cycle of faulting, forgiving, faulting, and forgiving is a system failure. True forgiveness requires us to drop the lenses we have been using in the past to mask who we really are and instead own our stripes. We aren't bad people, but some of us have weak self-awareness. We can't keep repeating the actions we want to stop, call them mistakes, and then ask for forgiveness. If we are repeating them week after week, then we don't really want to stop, do we? To truly forgive ourselves, we need to own our decisions and accept them as they are. Then, we need to correct our behavior.

The need to punish ourselves and others has been taught since ancient times. An example of the need to punish sins is the story of Prometheus from Greek mythology. He was the god of fire who brought fire to mankind against Zeus' desires. Zeus, the chief god, was furious and punished Prometheus for disobeying his orders by chaining him to the mountain and having an eagle eat his liver daily. At night, however, Prometheus would grow a new liver, only to be eaten the next day again. He was sentenced to a life of suffering because he was a god and couldn't die. It seems a harsh punishment for giving the needed fire to humanity. Prometheus did a good deed to all, but he got punished because he didn't follow what an old man sitting in the sky dictated. That's one of many ways humanity learned about God and the need to punish others. We followed the actions of an imposter god who is resentful, psychopathic, cruel, and tyrannical.

Unfortunately, religion has played a massive role in our inability to forgive ourselves. God, Higher Power, Creator, or whatever you believe to be a power greater than you doesn't hold a grudge and doesn't impose fear; humans do. She is full of compassion and knows that you did what you did because of the level of awareness you had at that time. Crimes against the Jews, Blacks, women, Asians, and other cultures or groups over the centuries are forgiven. We condemn those atrocities, but they are still forgiven. Although it may be hard to swallow forgiveness today, when an individual is assaulted to death just for being Black, Asian, or non-heterosexual, the Power of Compassion brings this understanding, which is only the beginning.

When we own our Power of Compassion, we learn that everything we did against ourselves and others deserves forgiveness. There is no need to pray ten "Hail Marys" and ten "Our Fathers" to receive the forgiveness of God in a confession to a priest who probably has done as many "sins" as everyone has. By the way, "to sin" only means "to miss the mark" and not what people think it means.

The Power of Compassion is also a gift from God to us. She isn't tallying our misses from the mark; we're the ones who do that. She doesn't even remember what we did; we do. We are the ones holding the grudges and holding ourselves back from forgiveness. When you know your heart's essence, you know God. When you know God, you don't miss the mark because there is no mark to miss. Open your heart to the Power of Compassion, and you can forgive yourself unconditionally. We can't do anything about the past, only what we do today. Remember, people with open hearts don't commit atrocities. It's not that complicated; we must connect with our hearts.

Can I Accept Myself?

I used to pretend I had green eyes and long, straight, blonde hair when I was a child. I pinned a bath towel on my head and swirled it as if it were the long lustrous hair I saw on TV and in magazines. What I actually had was thin, short curly hair. I hated my knees, which were full of scars from my many falls. I hated my curvy toe-nails and large breasts, which were too big for someone who was very skinny and looked like Olive Oyl from the Popeye cartoons, my friends used to remark.

We could argue that television and magazines have led women not to accept themselves. But have they? Women have been treated as a commodity since probably the beginning of time. We've had to be beautiful, young, and behave like a doll to get married. Most of our whole life's purpose was to be a wife and mother. The ones who wanted otherwise were judged and discriminated against. When you consider women's insecurity for the future, the doctrine of marriage, and the expectations imposed on women's behavior in history, you can see why any external traits that deviate from the fairytales are hard for women to accept. The TV and magazines didn't initiate it; they just perpetuated it.

The Power of Compassion calls us to accept our bodies, thoughts, and actions. Although marriage is no longer the goal for many women, being attractive still is. Nowadays, we have a broader representation of beauty, and self-acceptance is not only a must, it's a lifeline. This power is the necessary power for us to be fully alive. We can't be ourselves and have full, rich lives without owning ourselves and experiencing love as it was meant to be experienced: unconditionally. This power communicates through us and says, "I accept myself unconditionally first before I share my compassion with others."

Do You Practice Self-Compassion?

One easy way to find out if you practice self-compassion is by closing your eyes and dropping your attention to your heart center. It's that simple. Focus your attention on your heart. You may touch it with your hands or fingers to connect with the power.

Ask yourself: *Do I need to forgive someone who has done me harm? Do I accept myself as I am?*

Immediately, when you ask these questions, an image of some-one or some incident will probably pop into your head. If the im-age is of something that someone did to you, you need to forgive yourself first. It seems counterintuitive, but you need to release your expectations, resentment, or anger before you can genuinely forgive others. Remember, when working with compassion, you must have it in you before giving it to others.

Dig back into your past. I suspect that you won't need to go that far. My experience has shown me that people who hold high expectations for others have even higher expectations for themselves. They often have self-talk such as, "You are an idiot, stupid, loser, etc." Then, they run themselves ragged and com-promise their self-love to meet those unrealistic expectations. Again, before you forgive others, start forgiving yourself. Look at how you work, rest, eat, drink, have fun, keep your house, maintain your car, etc. This will give you a glimpse into how well you are loving yourself. If the results are discouraging, good. This is an opportunity to begin to practice self-compassion. Feel compassion for the way you have behaved toward yourself. Give yourself a little love today.

People with low levels of the Power of Compassion tend to see fault in everything. Their glass is half empty, and they sort through life for what's missing instead of what's right. Understandably, people want to improve themselves, but people with low levels of self-compassion seek to punish instead of learning lessons from the times they "missed the mark."

Mistakes aren't errors; they're just a change of perspective. For example, a wife opens the dishwasher and sees that her husband loaded the dishes opposite her preference with the plates facing right. She had told him before how she likes to load the dishes because her way fits more. So who is correct, the husband or the wife? The answer is neither. The Power of Compassion sees that the dishwasher is loaded, and both win.

Avoiding the Power of Compassion

Have you seen those gut-wrenching SPCA commercials with Sarah McLachlan? They were designed to touch your compassion with a heavy blow and motivate you to act. Many people will leave the room, close their eyes, or change channels to not see the images of the abused dogs. Not everyone has the heart to watch it. My young daughter Isabel used to leave the room because she felt so much for the animals.

Sometimes, people avoid feeling compassion for others because it's hard. These lovely people usually don't know how to process compassion because they don't know how to feel it for themselves. This isn't a fault; it's just an observation.

Compassion is painful sometimes. But when we feel it for others, we reduce each other's pain. So, avoiding feeling compassion doesn't help anyone. Plus, we need that discomfort to linger and expand compassion further.

When I was growing up, my brother found a lost puppy near our home. The dog had no collar, so my brother asked my dad if we could keep him. My father agreed. We named the dog Bookinha (don't try to pronounce it), but the English translation means "little book."

I liked dogs, but I didn't want anything to do with that dog. Our family of eight people lived in a two-bedroom apartment, and my intuition told me that we wouldn't keep the dog long. During the first week, the puppy peed on the floor, ate toilet paper, and chewed my dad's shoes. Each time the puppy misbehaved, my father hit her. I would leave the area so that I wouldn't have to see it, but I could hear the dog cry.

One day, my father hit the puppy so severely that she couldn't walk or leave the bathroom where she stayed. When my brothers left the apartment to play, she wouldn't go. That day, I went to the dog for the first time, sat next to her on the cold blue and white tile floor, and pet her for a long time. Bookinha was so sad and cried when I touched her. I held her in my arms, and I could feel her pain. I just wanted to take her pain away. From that day on, I began to spend time with her.

The following week, when we were at school, my father gave her away. He told us that he had found a home not too far from our house where she had more space. So we went to see her, and she got so excited when we visited her from the house gate.

One afternoon, when we went to visit her, her new owners told us that she had run away. We looked, but we couldn't find her. I cried and was sad for a while. Mostly, I resented getting emotionally attached to the dog when I had foreseen the outcome. I didn't know it then, but unconsciously, I vowed not to be attached to animals again.

Our pain is the door to our compassion. I have missed a tremendous amount of love by avoiding connection with animals. Women who have been hurt in relationships may refuse to open their hearts for a new romance, companionship, or marriage because they're afraid of a broken heart. This over-protection diminishes the Power of Compassion. Like many women, I, too, disconnected from the Power of Compassion to prevent pain. I didn't know then the benefits of opening my heart.

We grow compassion when we connect with people beyond the hello and weather conversations. We are genuinely interested in people's lives and not only the highlight of their social media feeds. People's hardship can be an opening for feeling compassion, but often, these moments aren't shared because we feel shame around our pain.

The Cost of Compassion

We cannot afford the price of avoiding our Power of Compassion. The cost is too high because it impacts our ability to live a good life. We are social beings. In adulthood, we may not need other people to survive, but we need people in order to thrive. A recent study on centenarians revealed that people who live past their one-hundredth birthday have a few things in common. One of them is that they have active social lives. They have meaningful relationships, and there's no question that compassion deepens all relationships.

Compassion expands and connects. It's also felt both ways by the person receiving and extending it. When a third party sees the compassionate exchange, they feel it too, and the circle grows. As you can see, the Power of Compassion is energy well spent.

Body, Mind, and Wisdom School for Compassion

Here are four ways to improve your Power of Compassion.

One – Forgive Yourself

To grow your Power of Compassion, begin by forgiving yourself for anything you feel you may have done to hurt others. You may need to go into your past, but don't spend too much time there. Just acknowledge those things. Every action you took happened because of your level of awareness at that time. You might have known better, but you did what you did because of your emotional state at that time. This isn't to easily let you off the hook, but it builds on your awareness and stops the heavy burden you carry when you feel guilty or wrong.

You may think you don't know how to forgive, but you do. All you need is to recall the times you hurt someone, tune into your heart to feel the feelings of compassion, and say that you forgive yourself.

Two – Learning from Mistakes

When you identify what you call a mistake, ask yourself, "What is this trying to teach me?" So many women unconsciously punish themselves over and over for something they did ten, twenty, or thirty years ago. I believe there are no mistakes in life—only opportunities to learn.

Three – Forgive Others

This can be a challenging one. Again, if you can't forgive others, you aren't forgiving yourself either. Forgiveness is not for them; it's for you. By releasing them from your space of expectation and judgment, you free yourself. You know you've forgiven others when you can lovingly wish them well.

Four – Tune into Love

Tap into your heart energy center, and feel the unconditional love from your inner guidance, soul, and spirit. Close your eyes, place your attention on your heart center, and reach for the love that is already inside of you. Stay there until you feel it. When you do, you will feel a Mona Lisa-like smile arriving in your body. It isn't unusual for people to cry when they feel the energy of love. Don't hold it in.

The late Louise Hay said, "Your thoughts are either beating you down or lifting you up." With the awareness and practice of the Power of Compassion, you are looking to be loved, first and foremost, by yourself.

Women who love themselves become extraordinary human beings who uplift the people around them. They go on to accomplish so much inside their homes, offices, communities, and many circles they stumble upon. Some of them probably are doing it already at some level and sporadically. But the most fantastic thing that happens when these amazing women consciously live their Power of Compassion is that they emanate great light effortlessly and unintentionally, uplifting the energy of everyone around. Their emotions influence their thoughts and words, and their actions grow in all types of waves of good deeds. Everyone loves being around them.

Chapter 5
The Power of Authenticity

"Women don't need to be perfect;
they just need to be real."

— UNKNOWN

"An old, old woman lived in the desert, and some even called her wicked, a hag, a witch, or the wolf woman, La Loba. She searched the terrain looking for bones, mainly of a wolf, and she sang over them, bringing them to life in the body of a wild woman."

You may have heard this story through the voice of Dr. Clarissa Pinkola Estes, the author of the book *Women Who Run with the Wolves*. Through stories like these, we learn what our ancestors wanted us to know: the spirit of women is wild, which means it's natural. We must be uncaged and allowed to be free.

Some people may picture a "crazy" woman dancing half-dressed through the streets with unbrushed, long hair, yelling songs of freedom. But that's only the spirit of a woman who has spent her life trapped. She needs that true wild expression of who she is.

The fifth Power of Women is the Power of Authenticity. It's located at the fifth energy center, which is the throat chakra. Energized by the color light blue and the sound element, the throat chakra begins to develop around our fifth birthday. It's also about our truth.

The Power of Authenticity is all about how we express ourselves in the world. It's our true voice. You can feel this energy. Just close your eyes, take three deep breaths, and bring your attention to the throat area. Sense if your throat's energy is blocked or open. If it feels tense or heavy, the energy is probably blocked. If it feels empty, the energy is open.

This power frees us from our inner doubts, releases us from our fears and reservations about our way of being, and helps us embrace ourselves and our truth. It also allows us to enjoy the blessings of our inherited qualities and the lessons we learned. This power celebrates who we are at our deepest level.

We learned in chapter three that while the Power of Confidence helps us step toward our goals, in this chapter, the Power of Authenticity gives us the "why to take the step" by aligning who we think we are with our authentic self. In that way, it inspires us to get out of our comfort zone and do the work we signed up to do.

When we're empowered in Authenticity, we color outside the lines and still show off our artwork. We witness this in our children, who have high levels of authenticity.

Authenticity is an amazing power of expression. It's beautiful to see people owning their uniqueness and sharing it with the world. On the other hand, this power is compromised when we become influenced by an agenda, usually someone else's. We diminish our strength when we walk on eggshells, bite our tongue, or silence our feelings. When we attempt to justify our dreams, we also reduce our authenticity.

But bear in mind that being authentic doesn't give us a free pass to hurt others or the right to call everyone on their bullshit. This behavior has nothing to do with the Power of Authenticity. Instead, it emanates from a strong ego with a hefty dose of insecurity. It's true that when we act authentically, people may not always like what we do. But the way we share our decisions or thoughts doesn't have to be an explosion of repressed, overdue reactions. We can be authentic with grace.

Of course, that requires practice. Few of us had role models to show us how we could be more ourselves. Most of the adults in our lives helped us build the shells we currently exist behind. I discovered that there are seven barriers to our authentic self, and we need to break through them to emerge as fully authentic. It doesn't matter how old you are. Your authenticity was likely compromised to a certain degree. How deep? Only you can know.

I found that most people have three or more shells that impact their ability to be authentic. They are beliefs we learned or acquired when we went about living. I invite you to explore each of the shells and decide for yourself if you have been caged by them.

Again, this is a personal process. If you find you have some of the beliefs, but they are *your* beliefs and don't limit your authenticity, move on to the next shell. You are the driver.

The Seven Shells

Here are the seven shells. Breaking through these seven shells will help you let go of the old beliefs that don't serve your authentic self.

1) Ancestors
2) Mother
3) Father
4) Lovers
5) Tribe
6) Religion
7) Self

Let's review them closely and improve our awareness of them.

1) ANCESTORS

The first shell influencing our authenticity is our ancestors' beliefs. It has to do with views from your family's origin—the behaviors, thoughts, and feelings that began in past generations and remain in place today. Because they've been around since before you were born, you had nothing to compare them to. Some of these customs may be well-liked by most people in your family, such as eating Sunday dinner at the matriarch's house or taking a family beach vacation every July. Others may include prejudices such as the dislike of Jewish or Black people, only marrying within the race or religion of the family, getting married by the age of eighteen, etc. Your job is to review your family traditions and beliefs and determine if any of the ancestor shells have kept you caged to discover your truth.

In my family, our ancestor shell was that we must work hard to have money and a good life. The stories shared in our house about my grandparents and their ancestors showed that you wouldn't have a good life if you didn't work hard. So I worked hard all the time. If anything was too easy, I had to avoid it because we believed easy work with money was a trap.

What is your ancestor's shell that you need to break through?

2) MOTHER

The second shell to break is the shell of your mother. Your mother is your first home, first connection, and first care. You trusted her. Without formal schooling, your mother begins to teach you from the womb. There was a theme in your mother's life that she repeatedly shared during informal conversations. This was her way of protecting you. In her mind, that shell would reduce your pain and, therefore, her pain because your pain was her pain.

If your mother worked too much, stayed in unloving marriages, ignored money, had affairs, etc., her story of struggle may become part of your shell.

My mother's shell was about independence. She told my sister and me over and over, "Don't depend on a man." Over the years, it was sound advice, but it cost a high level of trust in my relationships. Those types of shells caused us to find partners who can't be depended upon. What we desperately seek to avoid is what we will find.

What is your mother's shell that you need to break through?

3) FATHER

The third shell to break free from is the shell of your father. Your father is the first love for women. He's the man who protects us. For men, their father is the pillar to measure against. Sometimes, boys have a massive wall to climb. Other times, they need to descend to meet their fathers at eye level.

For girls, securing love from their father requires them to adhere to his rules. If he has specific ideas about how "good girls" should behave, we'll unconsciously act that way to get his approval. But the girls whose spirits run with the wolves may struggle to find their connection with their father. These free spirit seekers know where the shell boundaries exist and often break them. Then, when they come back full of enthusiasm and share their experience of freedom, they're often met with disappointment and a withdrawal of love from their father. If they cave, their Power of Authenticity begins to lose strength, and if they don't, they enter a journey of grief by losing the love and approval of their father.

Sometimes, the father isn't around, but there's still a shell caused by the absent man who didn't love and abandoned us.

What is your father's shell that you need to break through?

4) LOVERS

The fourth shell to dissolve is the shell of our lovers. One of the gifts of being a woman is our ability to share and connect with our lovers. This is a time when we enrich ourselves and the people around us. We are free to be the lover our spirit calls us to be. But our love partners have strong shells themselves.

How we love ourselves is how others love us. We bring our wounds to every relationship, and when we don't work on our shells, we also bring our ancestors', mother's, and father's shells to the relationship.

One of my clients shared with me that she got pregnant at seventeen years old to a boy who was twenty-one. She loved him, and they quickly married before she began to show. On her wedding night, wearing the beautiful white gown she purchased with the bit of money she saved working after school, she went to the bedroom and waited for him. It wasn't about the sex but the anticipation of the romantic wedding night she'd been dreaming about for a while.

The groom had been drinking all day. After all, it was his wedding day, too. When he came to the bedroom, he beat her senseless for no reason. Her mother had to take her to the emergency room the next day because she was black and blue. Later, he apologized and told her that his father told him to do it so that she would know he was the boss. They were together for a few more years, and she had another child with him.

Before you begin to judge my client, I'd like you to feel her pain. Feel what she must have felt that night and every other night her husband walked into their bedroom. Feel that level of pain, multiplied by the years of her memory even after she left him. That is the thickness of the lover's shell she needed to break. Since her husband, she hasn't been able to trust men.

Look at your past lovers, especially ex-husbands. They leave a shell.

What is the lover's shell that you need to break through?

5) TRIBE

The shell of a tribe is connected to the communities a woman lives in and around. These groups have expectations of how people need to behave. The tribe can be the people from their country, school groups, the neighborhood where she lives, church, clubs, or work environment.

Breaking through the tribe's shell may require courage. Many women exist in those communities without fully expressing how they think and feel about the boundaries the tribe has established. The need to be accepted by the group is an innate desire, even when the group is just an expensive country club.

Most of the tribal mind is exclusive, and the people are controlled by the group's beliefs. It could be the way they look, behave, speak, practice religion, display money, achieve success, raise their children, socialize, or even enjoy recreational drugs. The tribal shell will separate you from the group if you don't follow their rules, but there are no written rules for a tribe.

The shell may be related to the ancestors, mother, or father in a family setting. So, ideas such as women don't smoke or wear pants, can't learn math or study engineering may seem like simple shells to break when we look from the outside in. But the years of indoctrination in the tribal setting may lead women to believe in those ideas. And when they decide to smoke, wear pants, study math, or attend engineering school, they become an outsider. No one wants to be alienated.

As women begin to feel more assertive about breaking the limiting beliefs of the past, they use their willpower to march ahead and preach how old-fashioned those ideas are. Still, their inner being wants to be accepted. We all do. At that moment, many of us don't accept that we need to leave the tribe in order to free our authentic voice. Some will stay, and others will go.

Breaking the tribal setting may lead women to find other tribes and require them to do the work I list at the end of this chapter to accept themselves *over* the tribe.

What tribe shells do you have to break through?

6) RELIGION

Breaking the religious shell can cause the most disturbing and exhilarating acts of freedom, especially for people raised in orthodox religions that were widely accepted as the only truth.

I grew up in the Roman Catholic Church in a small town on Governor's Island in Rio de Janeiro, Brazil. We attended a small, unassuming white church that sat at the top of the hill facing the Guanabara Bay. Yet this one saved my family's life. It gave us meaning, activities, connection, food, financial help, and a foundation. I taught Sunday school, which was done on weekdays, played guitar during Mass, and participated in all social activities such as visiting the elderly asylums and orphanages, outreach to the favelas, organizing the St. John's festivals, and others.

Our church taught the concept of heaven and hell. We were told that we should fear God, who warned humanity through lightning and thunder in the sky, the Ten Commandments, and the concept of right and wrong.

Fast forward twenty years when I was attending a confirmation meeting at the local church in Rhinebeck, New York, for the parents of the teenagers who were two days away from receiving the sacrament of confirmation. This is when they confirm the decision their parents made for them when they were baptized before their first birthday.

A priest likely to be in his late sixties, dressed with an unfriendly attitude and a cold demeanor, affirmed that anyone who didn't attend Mass would go to hell. He was very different from the youth priests, who joked, played soccer, and talked to you as if you were a loved child of God. And the God I met in prayers and meditations, read about in books, and experienced as good and kind, would not send people to hell simply because they didn't attend long and tedious Sunday Masses. But, nevertheless, I didn't speak up when the priest made that statement.

That day, I awakened to my true faith and broke the shell of religion. I know that the God who gave people free will and equality wouldn't be a sadist SOB who would burn his children in hell if they didn't make the choice he wanted. That just made no sense to me.

However, when breaking the shell of religion, I caution you to look within and deepen your connection with your creator. I believe that religion and spirituality are two separate entities. One cages, and the other frees. I believe you can still find good in religion, but only as a place to begin restoring hope in the world, providing relief for the needy, and creating a connection with a higher power. Places that give us absolutes cut our voices, and our voices are gifts from God. All God's creation is meant to be free.

What are the religious shells you need to break through?

7) SELF

The seventh shell is the one we create with our conclusions. It isn't related to our families, communities, or religions but to our own thoughts derived from our experiences. These shells are beliefs we have about ourselves, such as "I'm ugly," "I'm stupid," "I can't cook," or anything else that destroys our self-worth.

These erroneous thoughts come from weak moments when we need to create some explanation for what's happening in our lives.

If a woman can't get a date, for example, she believes it's because of her looks. If she can't get a job, she assumes it's because she's stupid or incompetent. If she can't make friends, she concludes that it's because of some flaw in her personality.

If this is what you experience, I would like you to consider that your thoughts are creating your life. Women who don't trust men tend to find untrustworthy partners. Women who complain about people tend to attract people who give them reasons to complain.

When you identify and break the pattern of thought that puts you down, you'll open the door to your authentic voice, which will set free the energy you seek to attract.

What are the self shells that you need to break through?

Break the Seven Shells

The spiritual practice to break any of the seven shells that interfere with your authentic voice is a form of journaling meditation. There are five steps. Below is a sample of the exercise:

a) Identify the shell you want to break. Then, write it down in your journal or the book companion what you believe and how you act that perpetuates this shell.

b) What's your truth that's different from this shell?

c) Reflect on the cost to you of keeping this shell in place?

d) What's the cost to others of keeping this shell in place?

e) Create a new *belief* to break the shell.

The Practice

Find a place where you won't be disturbed for twenty to twenty-five minutes. Perhaps light a candle or burn incense. Set the intention to break one shell at a time. You can say the intention out loud or to yourself.

Grab your journal or the book companion and a pen and set them in front of you.

Close your eyes, and take three long, deep breaths. Then, say out loud, "This is a sacred space. This is a sacred space. This house is a sacred space."

1. Select the shell to break through. Using your journal or the book companion, write the name of the shell and what beliefs exist in that shell, how you behave as a result, and what bothers you about it. Write everything that comes to mind about the beliefs surrounding this shell. Spend some time there. There's no right or wrong way to do this. Whatever feels right is fine. You will know when you find the critical issues because you'll realize they've been a source of frustration or pain in your life.

2. Close your eyes and place your attention on your throat chakra. Ask for your truth. You can use your dominant hand to touch your throat. Once you confirm what you already know, write it down.

3. Consider the cost to you of not following your truth. Find at least three costs and write them down.

4. Consider the cost to others if you do not follow your truth. Find at least three costs and write them down.

5. Write your authentic belief. This is the part where you write down your truth.

Here is an example of how to do this practice. In this scenario, I am using the shell of the mother.

1. <u>Mother Shell:</u>

   My mother wants to control my life. She calls all the time and comes over unannounced. She's always telling me what to do. She criticizes the way I dress and buys me clothes I don't like. She thinks I can't take care of myself.

2. My truth: I'm a grown-up, and I don't need my mother to make decisions for me.

3. The cost to me: If I keep allowing my mother to interfere in my life, I won't be my own person, I will become her, and I'll live her life, not my own.

4. The cost to others: If I keep allowing my mother to interfere in my life, she won't deal with her issues, she'll torment me forever, and our relationship will suffer.

5. The new belief: Telling myself and my mother I'm a strong woman and ready to learn from my mistakes.

The Voice and the Lies

There's a story about the Voice who lived in the forest and was friendly and kind to everyone. Every year, the Voice visited the friends who didn't have the means to see anyone. One of her friends was the Mountain. So, every first week of spring, the Voice and the Mountain spent a week together, connecting and exchanging stories from the past year.

The Voice left the forest, charging up to see the Mountain, full of anticipation and excitement. On the way, the Voice met with the Lie, and they had a casual conversation.

"Where are you heading?" asked the Lie.

"I'm going to visit the Mountain," said the Voice. It's their annual visit. They have been doing the long week visits for decades.

"Ah, I thought you were going to the music festival by the village."

"Music festival?" asked the Voice with the puzzled look in her eyes.

"Yes, the Spring Music Festival is now held the first three days of spring."

"I didn't know that."

"It's a pity you're going to miss it. Everyone was expecting to hear you sing and share your songs with them. You know, you're one of the stars of the festival," enticed the Lie.

"I am?"

"Yes, didn't you get the invitation?"

"No, I didn't." The Voice looked a little sad and wondered if she was overlooked since she didn't get an invitation.

"Your picture is on the cover of the posters. We only added two of your photos, so no one would think we promoted you too much. You know, you're the only one allowed to perform all three days. People just love you."

"They do?"

"Yes. Why don't you shorten your visit to the Mountain and go to the festival? You can be with the Mountain in four days."

The Voice remembered the last concerts where she got a standing ovation, and everyone loved her performance. People threw flowers on stage, and there was a long line of people who wanted to see her. She was delighted.

"Oh, I'm not sure. But singing at the festival would be fun," contemplated the Voice.

The Lie got closer to the Voice and whispered in her ear even though there was no one around, "Would you rather disappoint one friend for three days or hundreds of fans for a year? Just tell the Mountain that you were sick with a sore throat or something and didn't know if you might make her ill. No one will be mad at you. What she doesn't know won't hurt her."

The Voice took a long breath, thought for a quick minute, and decided to go to the festival. She would visit her Mountain friend afterwards.

On the first day of the festival, the Voice sang beautifully and laughed with old friends. But at the end of the day, however, the Voice felt a bit guilty for ditching the Mountain.

On the second day, the Voice was the star. More people came to hear her sing and perform her most popular songs. At night before falling asleep, she felt a bit sad, thinking that the Mountain may find out that she was at the festival.

The Voice was so popular on the third day that they decided to extend the festival for one more day. It was utterly busy, and the venue didn't have space for all the fans who came to see her last performance. Although happy with the turnout, the Voice felt a knot in her throat when she knew she couldn't leave for the Mountain the next day.

On the fourth day, the Voice was terrific. She got a standing ovation again. She was the only one performing that day, and the show ran an hour longer because she also shared stories and how much she loved to sing. As the fans came in to congratulate her at the end of the show, she felt a bit distant from all.

On the fifth day, the Voice was exhausted. She wanted to get up early and head to see the Mountain, but she couldn't. She slept all day.

On the sixth day, the Voice left to see the Mountain and felt really bad that she shortened the visit by five days instead of the three days as planned. She didn't know how the Mountain would react, and she worried that perhaps their friendship would break or at least become distant. The Voice didn't want their friendship to change, so she began to think of the excuses she could tell the Mountain for not keeping their agreement.

When the Voice arrived at the Mountain, the Mountain was surprised. The Voice immediately cleared her throat and said, "I'm sorry I'm late, but I was very sick—too sick to send a message. First, I had diarrhea, then a sore throat, then a toothache, and a migraine. I stayed in bed all day. I feel really sorry, but I was just too, too sick. Even my back hurt. I tried to get up and force myself to come, but I was just too sick."

"I'm so sorry to hear that, my friend," said the Mountain. "I thought you went to the music festival because it's your favorite event of the year. But once I heard that the festival dates were changed, I didn't expect you to come at all. Poor thing. And you also missed the festival. Your fans must be devastated."

The Voice barely talked for the rest of her stay, and when she did, she had to clear her throat. On her way home, she worried that the Mountain would eventually find out the truth. Over the years, the Voice experienced anxiety and constantly had to clear her throat, which caused her to damage her vocal cords. As a result, the Voice never sang as well as she did in that Spring Music Festival.

* * *

This story represents women and the lengths we go to meet our needs without hurting other people's feelings. We might lie and walk on eggshells, covering our lies with other lies. Often, we use the "no one gets hurt" types of lies to meet our false needs. Going to a festival or staying home is a legit need. The false need is lying to avoid hurting the feelings of others when we have no control over how people feel if we take the path of our truth. Instead, we become disloyal to our authentic voice.

Over time, this behavior, which is regularly considered innocent, leads us to dishonor ourselves. For example, when we decline an invitation, we can say, "No, thank you, I can't make it. I need some downtime." Instead, we tell others that we are ill. We then anticipate how others may react, and we're often wrong. And even if they're upset, it isn't our responsibility to prevent their upset. We have a right to say no.

How do you feel about white lies? Unfortunately, even those seemingly small lies deplete your power. The biggest problem with lying is that we compromise our integrity. In other words, lying shows the universe that we don't honor who we are and what we want.

It may seem harsh to call little lies dishonesty when all we want is to have a quiet night instead of hanging out with people we don't feel like engaging with. Telling people we have a headache instead doesn't seem to cause any harm to anyone, but it does damage us.

The most significant detriment to the self is that when we lie, we tell our subconscious that we can't be trusted.

Teaching Children to Lie

The amazing Power of Authenticity begins to be compromised in childhood when children learn to lie to their parents, usually unintentionally.

When my daughter Erica was in the second grade, her teacher gave the class an assignment to write a few sentences and draw a picture of their family. She was six years old, so she drew her parents (my husband and I were separated), her sister, stepsisters, uncle and aunt, godmother, and god-siblings. When she turned the homework in, Mr. Smith, the teacher, corrected her that her family was only her parents and sisters, asking her to redo it. She came home that day and told me what had happened. I was furious at his lack of sensitivity and cultural awareness.

The next day, I went to the school to give the teacher a piece of my mind and a social lesson. In the Latin community, it's common to include extended family members as part of the immediate family. Immigrants in America also count friends as family. We call our close neighbors, friends, and even teachers "aunt" or "uncle." My main point was that we don't tell a six-year-old who isn't part of her family. He apologized, but my daughter was sad because she liked Mr. Smith a lot.

From that time on, my daughters were afraid to tell me anything that could get a reaction out of me. Both of them began to lie or withhold the truth. Now, who taught them to lie? *I did.* I didn't have to show them how. Like every human being, they figured it out on their own, but I introduced them to the need to lie to protect themselves and the people they love.

We all want to be loved and accepted; lying seems to be a small price to pay to keep our parents' love and acceptance. But unfortunately, when we lie, we diminish our authenticity power.

When we decide to become more authentic, we accept our choices and the consequences of our actions. Often, it isn't as bad as we think. It's easy to stop lying even if we have become accustomed to it. It only requires awareness.

Recently, I got invited to a family birthday party, and I RSVP-ed that I would attend. A few days later, I realized that I had double-booked myself with a commitment to meet with close friends. I mixed up the weeks. My first thought was to call my family and tell them that I was called into work. I didn't want them to find out that I preferred to see my friends. But after a couple of days, I decided to own my choice. I told my family that I double-booked myself and wouldn't go to the birthday party, but I would stop by to celebrate with them another time.

It wasn't difficult to tell the truth. I certainly didn't want to hurt anyone's feelings. I want the people in my life to feel valued and loved just as most people do. But our primary responsibility is to ourselves. That's authenticity.

Can You Afford Your Authenticity?

Would you sell your hand for a million dollars? How about one of your legs for two million dollars? Three million dollars for one eye? Most people would rather keep their body parts than have the money. Not being authentic is the same as not having an arm or a leg. It's a vital part of who you are, and no price can make up for it. You could still go on living without one arm or your authenticity, but powerful women would certainly avoid it.

When we don't authentically express ourselves, it's because of fear, which leads us to act in a way that doesn't honor our spirit. Some people put themselves down with phrases like, "I'm ugly," "I'm not that creative," "I'm goofy," etc. Begin to pay attention to when you put yourself down and make a mental note. Don't do it, even if it gets you a laugh from others. It disempowers you. Plus, your spirit knows your value, and those derogatory names are not who you are.

You may feel that you don't know who you are. If that's true, grab a cup of tea, play some of your favorite songs, and ask yourself, "Who am I?" Keep asking it multiple times. As you hear words like "I'm a mother," "a dentist," or "a wife," remember that these are your *roles*. You are not your roles in life. If you hear "I'm happy," I'm angry," or "I'm tired," remember that these are emotions. You are not your emotions. When you collapse all of the extensions of "I am _____," the identifications created to separate you from humanity and give you an assigned space too small to fit you, you become the *enormous* "I am." The *I am* is *all*.

You are a divine, eternal energy being, creator of ginormous expansion with a mission of living your purpose. You may not remember that you signed up for what people describe as *your calling*. But be still, and you'll remember it. It's only a few meditations away.

You are special. You are essential for the world. What you do is unique, and no one does it just the way you do. There is only one of you in the universe, and your power cannot be duplicated. You may have had parents, partners, families, and communities that influenced you to be someone other than who you are. But it isn't too late, and you aren't too old to be fully you. You can "unbecome" the roles, emotions, and even personalities that brought you to be the person reading this book.

Finding your authenticity is owning the spirit of your voice. What have you been trying to say to the world? What have you been trying to do? Could you awaken the spirit of your truth?

As you read these words, how do you feel? Can you accept your magnificent nature? Are you still questioning your level of grace because you may not have a career, a big job, or some type of special art? If you are, please stop. Don't identify with your roles in life or compare yourself to others. Don't even put yourself down if you feel you haven't yet determined your calling. There are millions of reasons why you are where you are right now, so breathe in this very moment.

Feel your feet and your hands. Look at them. Can you feel the area behind your neck? Can you be grateful for your eyes and the breath that keeps you alive?

Your life is a web. The millions of connections you've made and the ones to come have a universal understanding of your contributions to life, too grand to be fully understood. Perhaps you said something to a friend in high school that helped her avoid the wrong path. Maybe you offered coffee to a neighbor who got delayed going to the supermarket and avoided a car crash. Perhaps you signed up to be guardians of your children, who will grow up to make local changes with significant consequences in the world. The uniqueness of your DNA is not an accident.

Now that you are beginning to understand how brilliant you are, would you put yourself down or allow others to do it? Your authenticity power is your free and wild spirit that has nothing to defend or protect. Your freedom of being is fundamental to building the world we're recreating for our children and grandchildren.

Keep asking questions such as "What do I want to do?" "Where do I want to live?" "Are these my choices or someone else's?" "Am I over-compromising?" "What are my boundaries?" These questions will give you an idea of the level of authenticity you have and the starting point to become as authentic as you desire.

Remember Who You Are

To strengthen your power, you need to accept the woman you really are and release the need to explain yourself. Silence is a great and viable form of communication. Do you know who you are? Or better yet, do you know who you are becoming?

When we work with the Power of Authenticity, we begin to question choices we made from a place of outer expectations. This may lead us to end long-term relationships, move to another state, change careers, or renegotiate relationships. Divorce records are full of women who tried to fit into a role assigned by their parents, partners, religion, or their own ideas of marriage.

On the other hand, authenticity is the alignment of your thoughts and words with your actions. Get behind your desires, and everything else will fall into place. If you feel your goals and desires are too big or inappropriate for women of your age, race, looks, or education, you will sabotage your spirit.

When I got divorced after fourteen years of together, I didn't know who I was, what I liked, or what I wanted to do outside of finding peace of mind. This wasn't my husband's fault. Before being with him, I loved listening to Brazilian Bossa Nova music, going to the theater, watching documentaries, reading esoteric literature, playing guitar, entertaining friends, going to the movies alone, dancing, and more. About a year after my marriage ended, I realized that I had stopped doing all of those things I loved.

It took me a while to find myself again. When I finally did, it was a better version of me. I was more mature, confident, happy, spiritual, creative, and even looked younger (I have the pictures to prove it). Happiness and meditation will make you look younger!

It isn't unusual for us to forget who we are and what we want when we're very busy. Women have many priorities and a long list of expectations placed on us, and we've adopted them because our mothers did and their mothers before them. After all, we feel the need to be accepted by our lovers and communities.

But we women have a voice, and we need to express it for our good and the good of our families, communities, and the world. Make your expression count by being who you are or who you are meant to become. The power to express our authentic selves is priceless. We can't sell ourselves short. There have been too many people who have done that for us. It's time to be you—the one and only who will never be duplicated in all of history.

Your voice is needed in your home, schools, community, work, government, boardrooms, and everywhere women go. The world needs a female perspective on everything, and that's where you come into play. Of course, not every one of you will become the president of a nation, but how about your daughters and granddaughters? Perhaps you are opening the door for them to contemplate what is possible. Women are powerful.

Body, Mind, and Wisdom School

Here are four additional suggestions for you to improve your Power of Authenticity.

One: Discover who you are and what you want.

People are constantly changing. Life is changing. Nothing stays still. You must find who you are becoming now due to your learning, living, and detaching from your past shells. Consider that what you think is changing is just the release of the layers of misinformation you've held. Now, you're at a higher level of awareness. Ask yourself out loud, "Who am I? What do I want?" Keep asking multiple times until you know for sure.

Pull out your journal or the book companion and begin to answer these two important questions: *Who am I?* and *What do I want?* Write anything that comes to mind.

Two: Mind your words.

As you reawaken the Power of Authenticity, it will be necessary to mind your words. Women are known for saying, "I'm sorry" for no reason. If you bump into someone, of course, say you're sorry. But stop saying it when you need to make a statement, be heard, or ask for what you want. Also, stop discrediting yourself and relinquishing authority.

A few words to add to your vocabulary	A few words to remove from your vocabulary
I have a great idea.	I am sorry.
Would you be open to some feedback?	May I be honest with you?

Yes, and...	Yes, but...
No, thank you. I have previous arrangements.	... because I have a headache
It sounds lovely, but I won't be able to attend.	Sorry, I can't make it.

Three: Speak your truth.

I believe there are ways to say anything without offending someone or discrediting yourself. Speaking your mind is different from speaking your truth, however. Speaking your mind is often accompanied by frustration, anger, hurt, and maybe a long string of profanity. Speaking your truth is surrounded by peace. When you practice the Power of Authenticity, you work from your truth instead of discomfort.

Four: Stop lying.

When we lie, we don't fool anyone but ourselves. Yes, our parents taught us to lie, but we're grown up now. When we lie, we're attempting to be accepted, but our integrity is compromised. The moment we decide to tell the truth with kindness, our Power of Authenticity increases.

My dear women, release your voice. A strong woman with an authentic voice is powerful, beautiful, and timeless. You may think that what you have to share has been said before, but not the way you do it. Your pain is your cause. You can open the way or keep it uncluttered with your support. We are all waiting to see what you do.

Note: You can purchase the Nine Powers of Women Quantum Activation Program - Healing Through the Chakras #5: Power of Authenticity. This program is extremely powerful and will help you if you have a significant cause to share with the world.

Chapter 6
The Power of Intuition

*"Intuition is seeing
with a soul."*

— UNKNOWN

Many consider intuition to be the best superpower a woman can have. Many women acknowledge that they've felt it at one time or another and can understand the benefits of following it and the disappointment that comes with ignoring it.

Every human being has intuition, yet many people ask, "What is intuition, and where does it come from?"

I like to explain intuition as a gift from God, the Creator, or whatever Higher Power you believe in. Intuition lives where our soul resides, which is not in the heavens. The force that beats our heart and pumps our lungs is the same energy that feeds the essence of our intuition. And because we are spiritual beings having a human experience, intuition is in us.

I like to think that God took a long and deep breath, and on the exhale, she gave women the Power of Intuition. It was a moment of awe and inspiration. Then, she looked at the work women signed up for and felt content they had the tool to complete that enormous task. Intuition is a woman's partner.

Intuition is a power born from our sixth energy center or third eye. The sixth chakra of the body is located above the nose bridge between the eyebrows. It begins to develop around our sixth birthday, and it's energized by the color indigo or royal blue and the light element.

The sixth Power of Women is a divine one that gives us the ability to interpret energy. This energy center is responsible for supplying wisdom that we can't logically explain. It piggybacks on the heart center to help us process meaning. We didn't ask for this gift, but it's for our benefit. It gives us an increased level of awareness beyond what the eyes can see. If we choose to listen, intuition is the universe shining a light on our dark perceptions with clear and straightforward direction.

Intuition is also our connectivity with the spirit world, and I don't mean "ghosts." However, people who communicate with spirits have a more sophisticated intuition than our already fantastic one. I know that this may sound a bit woo-woo. But intuition is your ability to interpret the invisible world, and with practice, you can do what psychics do.

The natural intuitive nature of women is why we wake up before the baby cries at night, can sense when our children are in trouble, feel suspicions in our bones, and have premonitions that turn out to be true. When we connect with our intuition, we elevate our power to the wind.

Men have intuition, too, of course, but their left-brain dominance makes it harder for them to recognize the messages that their soul is trying to convey. Moreover, they often need concrete proof. So in many instances, they dismiss the guidance they receive, looking for logic rather than trusting their intuition, which some identify as a "gut feeling."

Left-brain-dominant women also struggle with accessing their intuition. People with this brain dominance tend to compartmentalize their world, see things in black and white terms, and seek a scientific explanation for abstract events that can't be explained in laboratories. But there is hope for everyone. With practice, accessing our intuition can become second nature. Even skeptical individuals benefit from improving their awareness of the world.

To clarify, women and men both use their right and left brains all day long, switching back and forth appropriately. But women tend to spend more time using the right side of their brains, which is associated with creativity, emotions, and intuition. Men who spend most of their time in the left brain are more analytical, logical, and objective. Being left or right-brain dominant is not good nor bad. One side isn't better than the other. The critical point here is that we all need to connect with our intuition, and we have numerous opportunities every day to do that.

Intuition Is Born

We are all born with a vast capacity level for intuition. It may seem that the level of intuition we develop around our sixth birthday begins to decrease in late childhood-early adolescence, but it doesn't. Intuition never reduces its essence. What decreases is our degree of connection with it, which impacts our ability to sense it clearly. Intuition is always available. When we're disconnected from our true source, we can't hear its guidance. It's similar to hearing a radio station. If the dial is between stations (out of sync), we can't hear the songs. In intuition terms, we can't access the messages that our intuition is trying to tell us. It's like the dial is between stations. But if we adjust it slightly to the right or left, we can hear.

The most common way we decrease our connection with our vast intuition is when our environment sets us up to change the dial even though we instinctively know it isn't the right thing to do. Our parents, teachers, and other influential adults begin to discredit our intuitive power with lies or beliefs that aren't aligned with our truth. They don't mean to, but it happens often.

Innocently, we begin to deteriorate our connection with the Power of Intuition. The way intuition is experienced in our daily lives is simple. We feel the truth with our heart, and our third eye interprets what we feel. In less than a microsecond, it organizes an understanding and gives guidance on how to act. We just know what we know, and this is pure, unobstructed intuitive power.

Because intuition is energy, it doesn't recognize space and time as the way of experience. Intuition can be in multiple spaces and times at once. That's why we're guided to take an umbrella, even though rain isn't in the forecast, or we have an impulse to call a friend out of the blue and find out they were about to contact us.

Most parents have no intention of destroying or diminishing their children's intuition. But they do it anyway. When I began dating after my divorce, I decided not to get my children involved in my romantic relationships until I was sure I was serious about someone. I dated a man for about a year who occasionally would come to my house parties. My friends and family knew we were dating, but not my children. My oldest daughter Erica was seven years old at that time, and every time my boyfriend showed up, she was mean or rude to him. One day, she opened the door for him and asked, "What are you doing here?" in an aggressive seven-year-old kind of tone. Another time, at the end of a house party, when most guests were gone, she said to him in an authoritative voice, "Are you still here? When are you leaving?"

Erica's intuition told her that my boyfriend and I were more than friends, even though I denied her intuition. She felt threatened by his presence, which is very typical for children of divorced parents. Unfortunately, back then, I wasn't as aware of this as I am today. I only told my children about the relationship because I learned that parents teach children to lie by lying to them. I didn't want my children to lie. Becoming honest about dating also helped them to trust their intuition.

Another way to diminish our connection to intuition is by staying too busy. Both children and grownups disconnect from their intuition when they're tired, overworked, and burned out. Having downtime helps us to be still and access higher levels of intuition.

How Do We Know We Have Intuition?

Some people don't believe in intuition at all. Instead, they seek proof or hard evidence of its function, and because we can't poke intuition in the eyes with our finger, they say it doesn't exist. However, we can deny the mystery behind the Power of Intuition if we ignore the miracles we experience and label them as coincidences.

As you read about the Power of Intuition and do some of the exercises, you will begin to feel a change in your connection with it. What you may have experienced as intuition will become less of a mundane experience and blossom into a divine intervention of your spirit in your experience.

Quite a few people believe that intuition is no more than signals we pick up in our brains. Many years ago, I told my boss's boss that I knew when I would close a sale or not. She said that I was just picking up signals from the conversation with the clients. Although that's possible, I knew it was more than that. I would already feel the energy around my clients early on in the initial meetings. Often, I would hear guidance to wait a day, offer this, or accept that.

People who were abused in childhood tend to have high intuition when they become adults. Trauma causes increased sensitivity and improves our ability to use intuition. This is because of the child's need for protection and survival. They learn early on to interpret energy through intuition.

How we use our intuitive power is up to us, but there's a vast difference between being vigilant, using intuition for survival, and thriving and seeking opportunities. Our intuition will warn us of danger, but filtering life through our intuition for survival will condition our power to look for trouble instead of sorting for happiness and success. When you diligently look for something, you will always find what you're looking for. So it's best to use our Power of Intuition for thriving.

I've worked with a woman who had been mistreated as a child for being very poor. Schoolgirls constantly teased Gloria for wearing the same clothes to school for consecutive days. She shared with me that she had only two sets of clothes. She was ashamed and tired of the abuse, so she often ate her lunch alone at the back of the school, away from everyone, to minimize contact with people. Gloria didn't make many friends and felt inferior to the other students. She was never invited to birthday parties, but she knew she couldn't afford to buy gifts for others anyway.

One time, the teachers got together, collected some money, and bought Gloria new clothes. She rushed home to try them on and show her mother, but her mom felt insulted and made her return the clothes. The next day, Gloria told the teachers that her mother said she didn't need the clothes.

Gloria didn't go to her prom either because she didn't have a dress to wear. One teacher offered to lend her a dress, but she felt she had to refuse because of her mother.

I began to work with Gloria when she was in her late fifties. She was distraught when she shared a work incident where she believed her boss discriminated against her. It all started when her boss praised two of her coworkers for a well-done job and didn't praise her. Gloria's coworkers usually didn't perform as well as she did. She was considered to be a top performer in her unit.

Gloria was beside herself during our conversation, assuming that her boss didn't like her and may have something against her. She was close to tears when she talked about it. She'd been in the company for some years, and even though her boss always treated her well and gave her good reviews, she couldn't understand what he had against her.

When we explored the event together, it was clear that Gloria's level of upset didn't match the events she described. So I asked her to look into her past and find a time when she wasn't as valued as someone else. That's when she told me her childhood story.

Gloria's experiences in childhood led her to feel inferior as an adult. She was still vigilant and sorting through life events that would trigger her feelings of lack. Her intuition stalled, so she wasn't reacting to her boss's forgetfulness or lack of praise so much as to her childhood feelings of being bullied and judged for being poor.

This wasn't the first time Gloria misinterpreted other people's behavior. Some of you may conclude that her intuition betrayed her, but intuition is always our ally. When we're stressed, we disconnect from the truth and instead connect with what we know.

In Gloria's case, what anyone would call intuition was actually her unprocessed wounds. We must understand that not every voice we hear is the voice of our intuition.

No one can access their Power of Intuition when they go into fight or flight mode. When we become stressed, we use our wounds as lenses. Our vision becomes narrowed, and we can't see our way out of a paper bag. It's a natural response. The negative voice committee in our heads amplifies our wounds. In those moments, intuition has no room to work its magic.

It's important to know that when we use the Power of Intuition appropriately, it will warn us of danger even though we aren't purposefully looking to avoid trouble. It naturally does it for us.

One way to confirm if what you feel is your intuition or wound is by asking yourself, "Is this me, or is this you (intuition, guidance, higher power, etc.)?" You will always receive the answer. If you don't hear it, then it's you, and you're working from your wounds. Feel free to ask yourself in your head or out loud. There is a sense of knowing the answer.

The best use of the Power of Intuition is to thrive. Having an intention to succeed helps you be mindful of your intuition and pay attention to what you want. Then, you can access your intuition at a moment's notice. All you need is to ask. Asking thriving questions will filter life for success. Asking surviving questions will screen life for pain. Would you rather have success or pain?

Using Intuition for Success

Let's agree that you would like to use your intuition for success, and success could be considered any positive outcome you want for any area of your life. To begin, you will need to convince yourself of your innate intuition. One way to confirm your intuition is to ask yourself, "Am I intuitive?" Even logical people can do that and wait for an answer. If your answer is "no," please go back and reread this chapter from the beginning. You missed some important key points. On the other hand, if your answer is "maybe," "I think so," or "yes," that means you heard your intuitive voice.

You may have begun to recognize that your intuition is coming through your self-talk, but not all self-talk is your intuition, of course. Again, how do you know the difference? Your intuition doesn't put you down; it only shares the truth. Some self-talk is the voice of fear, your parents' voice, your critical self, and your wounds.

Take a breath, and count from one to five in your head. That voice has the tone of your intuition. Try again to learn to recognize how you can discern your intuition from the other voices. There is no emotional charge when your intuition is talking. It's simple and will use short sentences with directions that are indisputable. Also, the voice of our intuition is peaceful and calm. It's easy to tell if you know how peace and tranquility feel. This voice doesn't push, fight, or judge. It doesn't focus on the problem. Instead, it offers guidance. It inspires and motivates. Please spend some time identifying your intuition's tone and message. It will serve you well.

The next step to using the Power of Intuition for your success is learning to ask thriving questions. These are questions that will move you forward. For example, asking, "What do I want to eat for dinner?" is better than "Do I want to eat fish for dinner?" The first question is a thriving question because it doesn't limit your choices.

Here is another example. Ask the question, "Where is the perfect job for me?" instead of "Is this a good job for me?" The first question will get you more guidance instead of a "yes" or "no" answer. You may hear the advice to stay a little longer in the current job before looking for another. Do you see a slight difference? Avoid questions with absolutes such as, "Is she discriminating against me?" or "Is he cheating?" Instead, ask, "What is the best attitude I can take right now?" This type of question will give you complete guidance. Also, remember, when you are upset or discouraged, you will need to elevate your emotions to calm yourself before fully accessing your Power of Intuition.

The third step to using your Power of Intuition for success is to trust the guidance you receive. Are you strong enough to listen to what your spirit knows is best for you?

Can You Trust Your Intuition?

The biggest impediment to fully benefiting from our Power of Intuition is trusting what we receive. We don't trust our intuition because the message isn't always the answer we want to hear. Even when we suspect the answer, it's hard for us to take action when the advice goes against what we wanted to do.

For example, Margaret's intuition about her boyfriend is that she needs to end the relationship. She has been considering it for weeks, but she doesn't want to be alone. So she finds excuses for his lack of commitment and disregard for her feelings. Every time she receives a nudge to end the relationship, she finds something to distract her.

One of the most extraordinary things about intuition is that it comes and goes without our asking. Margaret may ignore the first glimpses of her boyfriend's behaviors, but the next time he shows a lack of commitment or consideration, she will pay a little closer attention than the time before. Over time, she'll build the courage to take action.

The Power of Intuition is also patient. It will repeatedly give you the same message until you take action or the universe pushes you to the outcome. That's when Margaret's boyfriend will leave her for someone else or abandon the relationship without notice. When she's sad and angry, not so much about the end of the relationship but about how it ended, she will remember the many nudges she received from her intuition. Next time, she'll understand that she had the opportunity to walk out of the relationship instead of being pushed in such a painful way. Similar things happen with jobs, homes, and friendships. If you follow your intuition from the start, you'll reduce your pain.

If you have a hard time trusting your intuition, go back to the Power of Confidence chapter and reread it. Some women will need additional help trusting that inner voice and the Power of Confidence will do the job.

As I said earlier, the soft, brief, calm, subtle voice of your intuition comes when we're not stressed. Sometimes, the voice of intuition may show up in your mind a bit out of context. For example, you may be cooking dinner and have a thought to call your Aunt Clair. You pause to call and find out that she has been in the hospital. You may get up in the morning and think about checking your credit card. There's no reason for it, but when you follow your intuition, you find out that someone used it without your authorization.

People have similar examples with taking an umbrella, getting gas before the tank is empty, buying a book, and taking a different highway home. Later, they find out that those innocent, unexpected actions saved them time, money, and trouble.

Your intuition will not only rescue you from trouble but will also help you succeed. One of the best house purchases I've ever made was the result of guidance to stay with my final offer and stop any communications for three days. I purchased the house, spent eighty-five thousand dollars in renovations, and sold it five years later for two hundred and seventy thousand more than I paid.

The intuitive guidance we receive doesn't always come in regard to big things. It could lead us to a parking space in the mall during the holidays or a bargain purchase online. The key is to know we have it, be open to receiving and following it when we get it.

When Intuition Happens to Me

One day, I was on my way to work, and I had the sudden thought to take some of my *Women, Rice and Beans* books that were inside a box in my office. I didn't listen. That afternoon, I talked to a possible client, and the conversation about meditation came up. I felt the impulse to give her one of my books, but I didn't have any with me. At that moment, I realized that I had been guided to take the books earlier, but I had ignored my intuition.

Another time, as I was leaving on a business trip, I had the intuition to take a snack with me. I stopped at the door, turned around, and grabbed two protein bars. On my way back home, my flight got delayed, and I almost missed my connecting flight. There was no time to get something to eat at the airport, and there was no food served on the plane. My protein bars saved the evening.

People have used their intuition to close large deals, avoid financial losses, buy profitable stocks, end marriages, etc. My intuition manifests for me all the time. It can happen to you, too, and you can certainly use a spiritual ally.

Body, Mind, and Wisdom School

Here are four ways you can improve your Power of Intuition.

One: Practice It

One of the practices that will increase your intuition is taking action when you receive guidance and acknowledging that it was divine guidance. It isn't difficult to hear your intuition. The challenge we all experience is to trust it enough to act on it.

Once you begin to pay attention to the guidance you receive and confirm the benefit of acting on it, your relationship with your intuition will become better than you ever imagined. It will be the best ally on your path to success. Remember, your intuition is like a muscle that needs to be exercised, and the way you exercise it is by taking action on the little nudges you receive. It's that simple.

WE HEAR – WE TRUST – WE ACT – WE ACKNOWLEDGE.

When you act on your intuition and see the outcome, you improve your power. The more you see the connection between the sudden thought (intuition) and action (outcome), the more intuitive you'll become.

You can start practicing your intuition with simple questions about whether you need an umbrella or where you can find the best parking spot, but I would like you to stretch yourself a little by asking for guidance on something big or something troubling you.

The way you ask for guidance is just by being quiet and unphased by the events around you. First, meditate, pray, or do some spiritual practice such as concentrated breathing. Then, ask yourself the question and listen for the answer.

Initially, you will likely doubt what you hear. Was that your imagination? If that happens, ask again. When I ask for guidance for something with an outcome that I'm highly invested in, I ask myself, "Is this me, or is this you (divine guidance)?" And I hear a clear answer. Sometimes, it's me, and sometimes it's my intuition.

Once you confirm, be willing to follow through even if it isn't the direction you want to go. Remember, the tone of your intuition and the guidance it gives you will be soft and clear. Also, check in with your confidence. Know that if you're avoiding taking action on the guidance you hear, it may be that you're afraid. But your intuition will never betray you.

Two: Meditate Daily

Meditation is food for your soul. I encourage you to do it daily and not just once in a while when you become desperate for groundedness and a clear mind. Begin a meditation practice, where you set a time every day to quiet your mind. We improve our intuition by feeding the opportunities to be still with a purpose. Remember that it will be challenging to hear the soft voice of your intuition when you're rushing from one task to another, speeding through life as if it expires at 8:00 p.m. One of the benefits of meditation is that you will become less reactive to the "busyness" around you and the unplanned events that add a few lines to your to-do list. When you're less reactive to your environment, your intuition will surface easily despite any type of day you've had.

You can do a five-minute meditation. Visit http://www.ana-barreto.com/meditations to download it and other easy guided meditations.

Three: Use Your Throat Chakra

I consider this practice to be the golden nugget of accessing your intuition because it allows you to call on your intuition at a moment's notice and find true expression. Using the Power of Authenticity located in the throat chakra can help you reach your intuition and bypass any feelings that may be influencing you to not hear or follow it. Sometimes, we're afraid of being judged by others, and that fear blocks our intuition. Other times, we anticipate people's reactions, interfering with what we could hear from our intuition.

First of all, if you're feeling overwhelmed, stressed, or burned out, you will need to improve your energy by breathing deeply and slowly for at least three long and slow breaths. This will signal your body to relax. If you can't relax with six to nine deep breaths, do the nostril breathing in suggestion four.

Once your body energy improves, close your eyes, take a few long breaths through your nose, and place the four fingers from your dominant hand on the front middle of your throat just below your chin. This is your throat energy center responsible for the truth. Breathe two more times with your fingers on your throat and ask (out loud) your question for your intuition. Listen for the first thought that comes into your head. You may ask the same question again to confirm your answer. If you don't hear/sense/know the answer, you may still be stressed or anxious. Do the nostril breathing practice listed below, take some time away from the issue, and try again the following day or when you first wake up in the morning.

Often, people hear the answer, but if it isn't the answer they want, they say the practice isn't working. Remember that your intuition is on your side. Be willing to follow it because it wants to connect you with the larger part of you.

Four: Alternate Nostril Breathing

Alternate nostril breathing will help your body relax in ten to fifteen minutes and make it easier for you to access your inner guidance. You can also use this practice to relax when you feel angry, anxious, or have a panic attack.

Find a place and time where you won't be interrupted for at least ten to fifteen minutes. Sit comfortably with your back straight, if possible. You can select calm spa-like music to help you relax or go into the bathroom stall for privacy if you're in a public space.

Close your eyes. Feel the air around you and take a few regular breaths.

1) Using your right hand, close your left nostril with your pointing finger and breathe in through your right nostril.
2) Close your right nostril with your thumb, release the left nostril, and breathe out through your left nostril.
3) Breathe in through the left nostril, close your left nostril with your pointing finger, and breathe through your right nostril.
4) Repeat this pattern for at least three to five minutes.
5) Redo the practice, but this time, take a brief pause between each inhale and exhale.
6) Repeat this pattern for at least three to five minutes.
7) After some practice, do the steps without using your fingers.

Note: It's always best to start the practice using your fingers even if you know what to do.

Alternate Nostril Breathing

Two additional points come to mind as we close the chapter about your Power of Intuition. One, intuition does not impact outcomes; intention does. Two, intuition warns and guides us, and our intention sets the path.

Your Power of Intuition was never meant to be everything, so don't place all of your eggs in one basket. However, your powers are always available to you to help you improve the overall quality of your life. Having a clear intention of what a great life looks, feels, and tastes like will help you live it day by day with the help of your intuition.

All-day long, your energy expands and contracts. When we appreciate someone, it expands; when we criticize, it contracts. When we see beauty, it expands; when we see fault, it implodes. Because of this yo-yo energy, your intuition reaches you several times a day. Be sure to make time to love, laugh, care, create, be quiet, generous, kind, friendly, and look for any positive emotions throughout the day. Then, you can use your Power of Intuition to improve the quality of your life.

Your relationship with your intuition will grow over time when you hear and trust its guidance. So remember to always say thank you out loud or under your breath when you recognize the Power of Intuition at work in your life. When you acknowledge guidance, more guidance will come through.

Chapter 7
The Power of Beauty

"Beauty is not in the face;
beauty is a light in the heart."

— KAHLIL GIBRAN

In 1957, a group of monks relocated a giant clay Buddha to a new location in Thailand. During the move, the monks noticed that the statue had cracked. Later in the day, the head monk investigated the damage and saw a light emanating from the crack. He decided to chisel the statue, which revealed that underneath, the Buddha was solid gold.

It turns out that in 1757, the Burmese Army invaded Thailand, so the monks covered the golden Buddha with clay to prevent the Burmese from realizing it was a precious statue. Unfortunately, the Burmese killed everyone, including the monks of the monastery, and left without discovering the golden Buddha. Because no one was alive to tell anyone about the clay, the golden Buddha wasn't discovered until two hundred years later.

This true story illustrates the seventh Power of Women—the Power of Beauty. Inside everyone is a valuable being waiting to be discovered by the world. You are precious. When you discover your true beauty, you will be in awe.

The amazing Power of Beauty is born in the seventh chakra—the crown center of the body located on the top of our heads, and it comes to full force around our seventh birthday. This power is energized by the colors purple and bright white and the element of light. This power has little to do with your lustrous hair, glowing skin, perfect makeup, gorgeous curves, or attractive clothing. Instead, it's about how you see yourself, recognize your divine beauty and surroundings, and what you do with your essence, also called your purpose.

We walk the earth thinking and believing we are less than we really are until there's a crack in our world. This crack may come disguised as a crisis, a weekend retreat, an awakening moment in meditation, or a book. Then, we're led to see the beauty hidden inside us and recognize that this beauty is also outside of us everywhere.

The Power of Beauty is the manifestation of the divine laws through the presence of women. It's the power women use to create a beautiful life by knowing their inner beauty and their connection with the Universal Mind, God, Goddess, Higher Power, or whatever you call a power that makes your heart beat and your lungs breathe without your command.

You are a divine creation—beautiful, perfect, and "goddess-like." Would the creator make any being less perfect after creating the sky, the sea, the trees, and the flowers? This beauty is infinite and constant. You will grasp the vastness of your power when you become aware of the essence inside you and begin to use it for the good of all.

Your purpose is your beauty. Your beauty is your purpose. These two essences are directly related to how beautifully you will build your world.

We are all creators of the beauty of our lives. We don't do it alone. We have a partnership with this divine force inside and in every space outside of us. As you suspect, we are co-creators with the divine. We're in a partnership with the divine, but our free will makes each of us the leader.

Take a look around and see what you have created so far. I strongly caution you to avoid any harsh judgment of your creation. Before blaming God, your parents, partner, children, past choices, or your job, take a deep breath. Your younger self did it. She didn't have the level of awareness you have today. Use your inner eyes and be kind to the naïve self who has yet to understand the power you hold.

As the architect of your life, you have the power but not the obligation to create a beautiful life. You have at your command the

Universal Mind that responds to you by the way you think, feel, and act to create a beautiful life purposefully instead of by default.

Perhaps beauty may not have been part of your vocabulary or a desire thus far when you account for the setbacks of your early life. Maybe you don't know your purpose and the pathway to building a beautiful life. But as one of God's perfect creations, there are no mistakes in you, your life, or your goals. All you have lived so far has led you to this moment. It's like you were learning to test the waters to see which water you should drink more. To further understand this concept and your power, ask yourself, *do you see beauty in the woman in the mirror?*

Please pause and sit with your answer. Look in the mirror. There's great wisdom in the words, "Beauty is in the eyes of the beholder."

If you don't see beauty in the mirror, you aren't connecting with your divine self. Your outer world is a reflection of your inner world. To see beauty, you must see past the clay and find the golden Buddha, Christ, Shiva, Allah, or the higher power inside you. And if beauty is a matter of perception, and you don't recognize it in yourself and in your life, then you haven't connected with the divine woman who signed up to be in this lifetime and build a life worth living. In other words, you aren't aligned with your purpose.

Yes, purpose brings beauty to our lives.

You may have the most beautiful house full of expensive items in the best neighborhood, a handsome partner, and gorgeous children. And that's wonderful. But if you don't entirely like the beautiful woman in the mirror, you aren't experiencing true beauty in your world.

The daily news and popular magazines don't make it easier for people to see what's beautiful. We've been conditioned to look for bad news and places to blame. We feed our feelings with emotional outrage about the behaviors of humanity. But humanity is beautiful. Our nature is love, kindness, and pretty, but we tend not to recognize it because of what's being fed to us and what we choose to eat. We could complain about the news, but we have a choice to turn it off. I'm not suggesting we put our heads in the sand and forget about the world, but we can choose the amount of news we allow into our consciousness. It's hard to recognize the beauty in the world when we're bombarded with hate, disasters, and death. Horrible events are indeed happening somewhere, but not at the rate they're repeated on the news. A sure way to stop the promotion of one disaster is to have another one happen. Then, the new disaster bombards our homes because the television producers believe we want more of that. I don't think people want more bad news, but societies have become habitual consumers of unhappiness. Bad news, typos, outrage behaviors are shared more often than good news.

You may remember the events in America on September 11, 2001. Everyone remembers what they were doing when they first learned about the attack. The images of the planes hitting the towers in New York City played so often for weeks that it caused people to be retraumatized over and over. What was the benefit of that? Would anyone forget the impact of that destruction? I don't think so. It only led more people to believe that the world isn't safe, experience more stress than necessary, and forget to see what else is beautiful in the world. No one remembered what the sunset, moon, or waves looked like that day.

On the other hand, some good came out of that disaster. Extraordinary acts of heroism, communities came together, people became more compassionate with their families and neighbors, and the people directly impacted found their path to purpose.

Finding Beauty

It's not difficult to find beauty in the world. It may require you to disconnect from electronics. For once, look in the mirror. You are beautiful. Do you agree? Every inch of your body is gorgeous because of what is inside you. Let's do an exercise to help you rediscover your full beauty and what may be disrupting your vision. You will need to call your inner child and your Power of Creativity for this fun exercise.

Get your journal or book companion and draw yourself and your house. C'mon, you first drew yourself and a house when you're three or four years old. And that was pretty awesome. You still know how to draw. Get markers and crayons and try to use the right colors. When my younger daughter Isabel used to draw herself, she would use orange to color her hair. People used to tell her that she had beautiful red hair, and she corrected them, "My hair is orange." It was that bright orange.

Take your time and make sure you draw as many details as you can. Then, I want you to make a heart on every part of your body that you don't like or have hard judgments about. For example, if you don't like your breasts, draw a heart on that area. If you don't like your legs or hair, do the same. I want you to become aware of every misperception you have about your body.

Using your intuition, can you see why you don't like those parts of your body? That was the old you. Now it's the time to find the beauty in them. Every inch of your body has a purpose; therefore, it's beautiful. Find the beauty in the clay so you can see your inner beauty light up your life.

Next, draw a house. You still remember how to use triangles, rectangles, and squares. Then divide the inside of the house with the number of floors or rooms you have. Now think about your actual house and draw a heart on the rooms you don't like. For example, if you don't like the bathroom, write "bathroom" on one square and draw a heart on top. If you dislike your backyard, front yard, or kitchen, do the same.

Your space is beautiful. It's a reflection of your energy. We can paint a room, buy new furniture to make our space more beautiful. But if we feel negative emotions about the rooms, it's not the rooms; it's in you. You will not make your space beautiful until you find beauty in yourself. If you love your home, great job being beautiful. If not, you are only one drawing away to change it. Do the exercise. It's simple, but it works. Our minds think in pictures, and it's the shortest way to change your mind.

Finally, write the beauty equation at the top of the drawings:
Heart = Love

Music is a Path to Beauty

Another way to connect with the beauty all around us is through music. Music helps us to link with very high or low emotions. Music that brings us to more heightened emotions will elevate us to beauty. Music that is sad, depressing, or signals us to remember unhappy events will part us away from the beauty.

Music has a way of storing moments in our memory. When we hear a song that played at our wedding or the theme song of a movie we watched in high school with our besties and even the music we danced to at prom, it will transport us to a moment of beauty. It happened some time ago, but when we connect to the emotion of music, our body, mind, and spirit don't know when it happened; it only knows that it is beautiful "in this time."

Music is creativity drops dancing in the ether blowing beauty in the air. So, play your favorite uplifting songs as often as you like. I always play my music when gardening, cooking large meals, driving, riding my bike, or walking alone.

Feeling uplifted is not only good to connect with beauty, but it is also good for your health. Music has been shown to positively reduce pain, anxiety, and stress. In addition, research has shown that music can also have a profound effect on people by aiding in heart, mental, and physical conditions and even helping patients recover faster from surgery with less pain.

Play your music; your body will love you back.

The Life Compass

We are all born beautiful. You see babies looking at themselves in the mirror, and they want to kiss the mirror, touch, and hug themselves. They see animals and want to touch, kiss, and take them home. This is our natural state of beauty. As we grow, we begin to lose our innocence, hiding it with clay to avoid exposure to pain.

It all starts mostly by osmosis when we learn from the people around us. Our parents are the first culprits. They are masters at protecting us by introducing and projecting their fears onto us. They tell us things like "Don't climb trees," "Don't run on the street," and "Don't walk far from home because bad things can happen." They sound like useful advice because we don't want childing getting hurt. Unfortunately, these cautionary statements also introduce fear, impacting children's natural ability to follow their beauty compass.

You see, the Power of Beauty does indeed work like a compass, directing us to live and create beautiful lives. Some of you may suspect that your compass must be broken. As you look around, you may feel that you don't belong where you are, and you can't see a way out of your dissatisfaction. Perhaps you don't like where you live, and the conditions you've been subjected to are pretty bad. Or on the other side, you have a good life but feel something is missing. You still may not know what you want to do with the rest of your life. But every compass works. Again, if you aren't seeing your life's beauty, then you're simply disconnected from your purpose for now—something that you can absolutely rectify.

Around our seventh year of life, we already understand the essence of our purpose. At that time, we verbalized how we planned to create a beautiful life for ourselves. "I want to be a teacher when I grow up," we might have said. Unfortunately, more often than not, children are misdirected by adults struggling to create their own beautiful life. Their confusion teaches us not to trust our own knowing. They might say, "Teachers don't get paid enough," "Nurses aren't doctors," or "Go for the real money." Although well-intended, our parents ask us to trade our life's purpose for security. And it isn't a fair trade.

Because as children, we want to be accepted and loved and don't want to disappoint our parents, we forget our initial dream when we sense their disapproval of our future plans. It's okay to ignore the desire to be a teacher, but not the essence of working with children. The child who wanted to be a teacher may end up working in another industry, feeling unhappy and stuck, distrusting their longing.

As we get older, life often reminds us of the purpose we signed up for before we were born. Perhaps we see a teacher helping a student or a nurse caring for the sick, which causes something to be sparked within us.

As an adult today, you may believe that several circumstances must change before you can fulfill your purpose and see beauty in your life, but you're misinformed. The Power of Beauty calls us to seek small wins before the larger ones can be fully seen. And for this, you need to be aligned with your purpose.

When I ask clients who are struggling with their career what they wanted to be when they were kids, most of them can't remember. I ask them to ask their mothers, but their moms don't remember either. Still, questioning our parents often triggers memories. When we receive negative feedback from our parents, we tend to forget the specific negative experience, but it's stored in our minds.

These days, too many people have second and third careers. I suspect that many of them initially followed the security path until something happened. Perhaps they were fired, downsized, or just had enough of their unsatisfactory work. When older and wiser, people discover their need to live a life that makes them happy, and true beauty and purpose make people happy.

The Beauty of Your Purpose

Our Power of Beauty directs us to our natural ways of being: love, happiness, and connection. When we follow our true happiness, beauty shows up. It has to because we're connected with our essence. This pure energy is always available to those who feel their divine beauty in their core due to their alignment with spirit. It seems like it's an unusual mystical experience, but it's as physical as it can get.

You see, hear, or sense the guidance to a path directing you each step of the journey. It doesn't mean that you won't experience the thorns and the walls. But once you choose to embark on the path of your purpose, doors do open. There will be obstacles, but they are there simply to slow you down enough and help you remain absolutely clear about the calling you've answered. This also teaches you patience.

The longer you stay on the path, the easier things will become. At one point, you'll know that you answered your calling because purpose will bring you back to your Power of Authenticity. You will see your true beauty then.

I like watching the tall trees being shaken by the wind and their leaves shivering in the air. Beauty sees them in excitement, celebrating their purpose. If you mistrust what you see, you will call it the wrath of nature waiting to take the trees down. You fear for your surroundings. While you are afraid for your safety, you miss that the leaves have waited to fly free and become part of the ground, the soil, and the nutrients for a new family of trees. Trees are a perfect example of living on purpose.

Your purpose is also waiting to be set free and become part of something larger than you. There are no limits to your purpose. It wants to be beautiful, and it's beautiful if you let it be.

Restoring the Power of Beauty

Here are six suggestions to restore your Power of Beauty.

One: Align Yourself with Your Purpose

When we think about finding our purpose, we think about what job will make us happy. But this thinking comes from a self-serving place. What's in it for me, how much money does it pay, and what are the benefits? Knowing your purpose and acting on your mission, which is how you express your purpose, will create beauty in your life. But your purpose isn't really for you. It's how you will serve the world. Let me repeat: your purpose is your way to serve the world. When you serve with your gifts, the talents you were born with, you live a life of meaning and happiness, which unfolds the beauty you seek to be and experience.

Plus, you don't "find" your purpose—you remember it. The question is whether you will trust it when you remember it.

Find out how you can serve, and you will know your purpose. Einstein, Steve Jobs, and Mother Teresa clearly had a well-defined and clear purpose. Unfortunately, some people may perceive them to have a ginormous purpose. Your bus driver, the grocery store cashier, and the school janitor may be perceived to have minor purposes, but that isn't true. All purposes are essential and require the same level of dedication. Can you imagine a day with no drivers or a school with dirty classrooms? It would be a disaster. Everything has a place, and everyone is needed. All purposes support other purposes. Plus, we don't know if what those people do is their purpose or a job. For example, the bus driver's purpose could be protecting children in a dangerous neighborhood or volunteering to serve dinner in a soup kitchen.

Two: Surrender to Present Conditions of Your Life

The practice of surrendering to the current conditions of your life will revitalize the way your feel about everything. This practice can be misunderstood as resigning or giving up, but it isn't. Surrendering stops the fight against yourself, and fighting yourself isn't worth the time or effort. Simply put, you created what is, and now you're ready to build something else.

As you read these words, take a deep breath, release it, and let your shoulders drop on the exhale. Do this three times so that you can begin to surrender. Yes, surrendering begins with each conscious breath.

If you don't like your job, for example, accept that and surrender it in a breath with the help of your shoulders. If you don't like where you live, accept that and surrender. Do you dislike your partner? Accept that and then surrender. I want you to surrender to what you've created so far. It's only temporary.

I ask you to practice three days of surrendering. Just find a quiet space, sit comfortably, and do nothing for twenty minutes except to breathe in and out. With each breath, let go of any conditions in your life that you don't like. Use your shoulders to help you surrender, and don't seek solutions. Let the answers come to you. Don't worry if you don't immediately recognize a way to solve it. You'll hear the resolution soon.

This practice of surrendering will improve your energy. The fight against the things you dislike only keeps you exactly where you are and creates more of what you want to leave behind.

Surrendering is the art of *trust*. Believe that there's an immense intelligence behind your ability to create beauty in your life.

Three: Stop Complaining

Stop complaining about everything you dislike in your life. You'll no longer talk about your boss, pay, landlord, or anything that sparks dissatisfaction in you. This is another form of surrendering. If you think about something that upsets you, stop giving more power to it by speaking about it out loud. When the thought comes to mind, say to yourself, "I surrender." You can do this practice at any time. When you stop complaining, your awareness will be open to happiness, which is the beauty you seek.

Four: Allow Yourself to Be Brilliant

To rebuild your Power of Beauty, give yourself permission to be brilliant. This means you will stop doubting your ability to build the life you've dreamed of. It isn't too late, and you aren't too old.

If I asked a room full of adults if they believe they're brilliant, few would come forward. If I asked the same question to a classroom of seven-year-old children, most of them, if not all, would eagerly raise their hands and tell me why they're stars.

When we think of brilliance, our brains race to find all the reasons we can't possibly be brilliant people. We equate it to highly talented and famous individuals like Oprah Winfrey or Martin Luther King. In Britain, people often use the word "brilliant" to characterize good deeds, smart actions, or good ideas such as suggesting a pub with a great beer. British people have found the true meaning of "brilliant" in an amazing way by including everyone.

I want you to know that your divine nature is waiting to glow. Your brilliance from the age of seven still exists inside, even if you're now seventy-seven. You can own it by stepping into your purpose, whatever that is. You don't need to quit your job or wait to win the lottery. You can start by doing what gives you joy a few hours a week. Release any expectation. You've already surrendered to your current job and everything you've been complaining about. In doing that, you've created beauty in small doses. Say to yourself out loud, "You are brilliant! You are beautiful! You are creating a beautiful world for yourself!"

When I ask you to allow yourself to be brilliant, I'm asking you to remove the outer layer of your being and let your divine self shine like the golden Buddha. Your divine cut is unique, like a diamond. No one can shine just the way you do; you are precious.

There are multiple ways to shine your light in the world, but you can radiate the light that exists inside of you only when you accept your brilliance. Your light is unique. There are many wise and talented people, but they are somewhere else, and you are here right now. There's much that you can do just from the space where you live. Write, paint, sing, bake, teach, do crafts, share your joy. Start small and see where it goes.

Another way to accept your brilliance is to remember how you used to feel before you forgot your bliss. You can tap into the feeling when you look at your childhood pictures and remember how you felt. Pull out your old box of photos and remember your eagerness and wisdom. Just like your purpose, your radiance isn't self-serving; it's for the world to see. The more people shine, the better and more beautiful our world becomes.

Five: Ask for Divine Help

Feel free to ask for guidance from the divine world. Remember, you are co-creators. Jesus, Angels, Goddess, God, Divine Mothers, ancestral grandmothers, and any spirit of light can lead you to the beautiful path you seek. But they won't interfere unless you ask for their help. So trust the voice that may seem like intuition, a gut feeling, or a strong pull in a specific direction. The spiritual world is helping you.

Release your skepticism. There are miracles we can't explain. Why do you need an explanation if you get the results you want? You don't need to share with anyone what you do when you meet the cushion of your spiritual practice or the bench of the church you visit. There is only one requirement to get spiritual assistance, and that's faith.

Faith will allow you to notice the help. And when you do, say thank you. As you ask for help, you will be saying thank you so often that these two words will be regulars in your vocabulary.

Six: Do the Drawing Exercise
While Playing Your Favorite Music

The drawing exercise introduced in this chapter may look like child's play, but it's powerful. I would like you to draw yourself and your house while playing music that uplifts your soul. Because it will access your inner child, who remembers how beautiful you are, and your critical adult self, the drawing with the hearts will influence your subconscious to accept your brilliance and beauty. Also, the music will anchor you to the moment of transformation. Every time you listen to the songs playing while drawing, it will reinforce the understanding that you are beautiful and there is beauty in your life.

Remember, the moment you recognize your beauty, you will drop the lens of your limiting conditioning. Then, the world will reveal itself as the beautiful place it has always been. I am waiting to see your brilliance.

Chapter 8
The Power of Generosity

*"Generosity is the most natural outward expression
of an inner attitude of compassion
and loving-kindness."*

— THE DALAI LAMA XIV

Generosity is remarkable. Here is an old tale about her that explains this power for humanity. (Yes, Generosity is female.)

Generosity walked through the door and announced to the people in the house in her lovely singing voice, "I'm hooome!"

The people in the house heard her, and some looked at her for a second, nodded, and went on minding their business.

Generosity put her belongings down where she usually left them. Then, filled with optimism and enthusiasm, she greeted each person in the home. Each individual politely greeted her back, but they quickly returned to their affairs, thinking she was a bothersome little bugger. They didn't want to engage in conversation.

Generosity opened the windows to let in the fresh air. The people in the house were a bit annoyed at first because bugs would come in. They rolled their eyes but let her do her thing. Soon, they enjoyed the light breeze that traveled through the house. As a result, they took longer and deeper breaths.

Then, Generosity began to clean the house. She vacuumed, mopped, dusted, and washed everything that needed attention. The people felt inconvenienced by the loud vacuum and the need to lift their feet – you could see it in their faces – but no one said anything. As soon as Generosity finished, the people looked at the house and felt relaxed and more comfortable in the clean home.

Later, Generosity cooked a meal, opened a bottle of wine, and invited the people to the table. Of course, they wanted to eat in their regular spots alone in front of a computer or television. Still, with her pleasant demeanor, she convinced them to come to the table she set with fresh flowers, nicely pressed linens, and beautiful china. They came, admired the table, ate, and enjoyed the meal. When each one finished eating, they quickly left their seats in the dining room to not help with the dishes. Generosity cleared the table, washed the dishes, and tidied up the kitchen. The people didn't even notice.

Lastly, Generosity made some tea, stretched herself on a lounge chair with comfortable pillows, opened a book, and connected with the sunset. She was as happy as anyone could be. The end.

* * *

Many individuals would be infuriated by the people's actions in this story. They didn't help and never said thank you. But Generosity never asked for help, and she didn't stress out or get overworked about it.

Some women might recognize themselves in this story until the time after tidying up the kitchen. Then, instead of finding something relaxing to do, they would be upset about the lack of help. It's understandable, of course. Women work longer hours to do nice things for the people in their lives, and too many times, no one helps or says thank you.

The people in this story represent our environment and the community we build, however. Generosity is our in-spirit service to others. It's a state of the heart, not the mind. Generosity doesn't require recognition, although it's always appreciated.

The Power of Generosity spins from a small heart center located in the palm of your dominant hand. It's also called a small heart chakra, and it's energized with the colors green, pink, and bright white. Some people can feel a little tingling in the center of the palm of their hand when they are either being stingy or over-giving. This usually means that your Power of Generosity needs some attention. It doesn't necessarily translate that you have to give to others. It could also mean that you need to be generous to yourself.

True generosity is inspired. You want to do it. It's irrelevant whether people recognize or enjoy your good deeds. As long as what you do doesn't deplete you and you aren't using it to manipulate or control others, generosity serves you well.

Balance for the World

The Power of Generosity is our ability to give to others without hurting ourselves and allowing others to be generous too, not out of obligation, but from an open heart. This power is unique because it encourages us to balance giving and receiving in the world.

When we talk about generosity, many people believe that we must take from the people who have "too much" and give to those who don't have enough. But the Power of Generosity calls on us to open our hearts and give what we feel inspired to give.

Giving isn't only to be done for people who have less. This simple perception of "more" and "less" is an inconsistent observation that requires comparison. Every time we engage in comparing one against another, three people lose—including you, the judge. Generosity doesn't associate with any evaluation.

The Power of Generosity invites us to release any judgment and open our hearts. This is when inspiration shows itself in a nudge, calling us to be generous with our time, money, possessions, or work.

As you continue to learn about the Power of Generosity, you'll be called to release any judgment about what generosity looks like and all of your assumptions about giving, having, and receiving. I've noticed that some people have strong feelings when they see a panhandler asking for money on the street or see someone driving an expensive car. If this is you, please be willing to hear with your heart, and then you can make up your mind.

One misconception people have about generosity is the belief that only one of the parties is the beneficiary of good deeds. But generosity is a two-sided act. First, giving and receiving go hand in hand. The person who receives is as generous as the person who gives. That's because the receiver is making the space for the giver to practice generosity. Second, the exchange makes it possible for both the receiver and the giver to feel good. The act of generosity has a tremendous physical, emotional, and spiritual benefit to both. Both giver and receiver are gifted with a great dose of dopamine, the feel-good hormone, and oxytocin, the bond hormone that helps reduce stress, improve mood, and create connection. The benefit multiplies when the gifts have an intended recipient instead of just dropping old clothes in a donation box.

To activate your Power of Generosity, all you need is to practice acts of kindness or receive help with grace.

The biggest obstacle to growing your Power of Generosity is holding on to things too long that no longer serve a purpose in your life. For example, you might still have an expensive dress that doesn't fit anymore.

Our basements, garages, and attics are full of old, broken, unused items that we can't part with. We tend to call them mementos, but they're just clutter that blocks not only our Power of Generosity but also the energy of abundance. Those items can also be called "fear." We project meaning onto these physical objects because we're afraid of letting go.

Perhaps you're trying to sell those items and recover some of the money you spent on them, but you haven't had a chance to take a picture of them and put a listing online. Maybe you rationalize that you may need them someday, and you just can't find the strength to give them away. The problem with this thinking is that items that were at one time a representation of spontaneity, fun, wealth, and prosperity are now a representation of lack.

The items not being used and occupying physical and energetic space in your life will hold you back from being generous with yourself. At this point, it isn't about donating to someone else who needs it. Spiritually speaking, it now becomes about your generosity to yourself and having a clear mind and heart with no more procrastination.

Physical clutter also clutters your intentions. For example, every time you open the closet, go to the basement or pass by the box of items taking space in the garage, you say to yourself, "I need to get rid of this." That thought stays in your subconscious, and it takes valuable energy that could be used elsewhere to benefit your well-being. So instead of having room for prosperity, depending on the amount of clutter, you may be screaming energetically, "I don't have space for what I really want or need."

So if abundance isn't flowing in your life, look at where you're holding on to things you don't need.

Take a quick assessment of your generosity level by answering the Nine Powers of Women Book Companion questions.

How to Let Go with Generosity

The two words "letting go" are often said but rarely practiced. I suspect that some people don't know how. It's like we have two little people sitting on our shoulders. One says, "Let it go," and the other says, "What if you need it tomorrow?"

Letting go is a decision, and not letting go is also another decision. Every choice has a belief attached to it, but many people aren't conscious of the beliefs standing in their way. One of the common thoughts behind not letting go of things we don't need is that we don't have enough. People who struggled financially in childhood tend to numb their past struggles by accumulating things.

If you have rooms, a basement, or a garage filled with things you can't seem to let go of, the practice of generosity is calling you.

First, ask yourself: *Do I want to have more generosity in my life? Do I want to lift my energy and have the strength to do the things I love? Do I want to increase my abundance?*

If you answered "yes" to any of these questions, it's time to release the chains holding your Power of Generosity hostage.

Of course, if you're a hoarder, you will need professional help. Please don't do it alone. Getting help is an act of generosity with yourself. But remember that your friends and family may not be as sensitive as you need them to be during the process. They may have good intentions, but they might have run out of patience and are likely to criticize. You mustn't feel judged.

If your clutter isn't bad, select one room at a time to declutter. I always recommend that you start with your bedroom. The spaces where you spend the most time will improve your energy and help you tackle the monster that tends to be the basement, garage, or attic.

The Bedroom is the Kingdom

As I said earlier, the bedroom is the most important room in your home if you sleep there. Begin by removing all the clothes in your closet and dresser. Next, remove all the books, magazines, boxes, and paper. You can leave the bed, nightstand, and dresser.

Clean every surface of the room. Vacuum, mop, dust, wipe the walls, windows, everything. Wash the curtains and clean the shades. Get new sheets and bed covers if you can afford them. This will signal your subconscious that you are making a new beginning.

Start bringing the clothing back, but only those you love and truly fit. Don't try the clothes on, however. It will take you off track if you begin to try them on. So instead, put the clothes you don't like into a bag labeled *Donations*. As you do, say mentally or out loud, "As I practice generosity, I honor my Power of Generosity."

Place the ripped or worn-out clothes in another bag labeled *Garbage*.

Next, put the clothes you are uncertain about in another bag labeled *Generosity*. These are the clothes you will try on after you have finished cleaning and organizing the bedroom. Again, don't try them on until you have completely finished for the day. The *Generosity* bag is the gold. You have some attachment to these.

Another rule that helps you decide what to keep is to part with anything you haven't worn in the past year except special occasion clothes. If the items don't fit, need repairs, or are too worn, get rid of them.

Do the same with shoes, purses, jewelry, and books. Recycle your magazines. If you saved the magazines for research and recipes, place them in a box. Give yourself two weeks to cut out anything you're interested in. After that, recycle them whether you had a chance to go through them or not. You can have one small or medium-sized basket in the room as a catch-all bin so that you don't keep things on the floor.

If you don't have a nightstand, get two. You can buy used ones and place one on each side of your bed. It will serve as additional storage for books and souvenirs. Also, having two nightstands is an energy cure for relationships. You want to have things in pairs in the bedroom.

Make sure there's nothing under your bed. If you have a storage drawer under the bed, make sure it isn't too full, and check it for old and ripped linens. You can dispose of them in the labeled bags.

Check for the subliminal messages that the pictures on the wall convey. Ensure that those messages and imagery are positive ones.

Once your bedroom is ready, you should have a pile of things to try on, another pile to donate, and one to dispose of. Try not to overthink it. Your goal is to become more generous and make room for abundance by creating space in your closet, drawers, and other storage compartments.

Try to eliminate everything within twenty-four hours. If you don't know anyone to give the items to, place them in your car and drive them to the closest donation center right away. If you want to restart your abundance, you can ask for a donation form and use it as a tax deduction. Remember that abundance isn't only about money coming in but also about less money going out.

The items you want to sell need to find a home outside your bedroom. If you don't sell them within two weeks, donate them.

The items you still want to try on will extend your generosity. Make an agreement with yourself to part ways with half of those items. I won't send the clutter police to your home, but try to honor this process.

If you're still struggling to let go of things, visit my website at http://www.ana-barreto.com/meditations, and listen to the Willow Tree Meditation for a few mornings. It will help you release attachments.

My Practice of Generosity

When I was married, I used to host my husband's family and our friends for the holidays. We had as many as twenty-three people at a time. I loved to entertain and had fine china, crystal wine glasses, cloth napkins, and other items to set a beautiful table. I even set the table three days before the dinner. When we got divorced, many of his family members cut ties with me. Our holidays were smaller, and I also moved to the countryside. Not too many friends would drive that far.

In 2008, during the recession, my business failed. I didn't earn enough money for six-plus months. In that time, I depleted my savings, was late on my mortgage payments, and maxed out most of my credit cards. I had to sell my house, get a job, and find another place to live. As I was getting the house ready to go on the market, I received the message during a Tao Reading that I needed to let go of anything that was old and spoiled. In other words, declutter. I tried to do a garage sale, but in the country, very few people showed up. My children made more money by selling lemonade those two days than I did selling my old items.

So I packed half of my precious china, kitchenware, my marital bed in the guestroom, and several household items to donate to the women's shelter. I even paid to have the large items taken to the house of a victim of domestic violence. I also gave all the jewelry my husband had given me during our marriage to my daughters and stepdaughters. It felt great to let go of the expensive things I had and no longer needed.

Since then, I have decluttered my life two to three times a year. These days, rather than give me a gift, I ask family and friends to donate to the women's shelter. Even so, I still get presents. The Power of Generosity calls for us to make space to receive, and gifts often come unexpectedly. If you feel that you have everything and can buy what you need and want, please remember to make space to receive. You're allowing others to be generous with you.

The Best of Generosity

The Power of Generosity involves more than giving and receiving. Another area that is equally important and needed by humanity is the ability to use our natural gifts. When we're born, we agree to contribute to the expansion of humankind with our talents. For some, it's to paint; others play music, write, cook, raise children, teach, and bring light to others.

Many people believe that having talent means being a famous painter or actress on television and in movies, but this isn't true. Everyone has talents, and we don't have to share them with all eight billion people on the planet. You may only share your talents with your community. You can go as wide as you're called to and want to, of course. What you do with your talents is encompassed into your free will.

But keeping your talents hidden is the opposite of generosity. At this time, sharing your gifts isn't tricky.

Over the years, many of us have bought into a belief in scarcity, which is that only a few people find their true calling, know what to do with their lives, and can support themselves in doing it. The need to earn a living may have derailed our minds and hearts from our purpose and mission. If this reflects your experience, please don't despair. You may not be as off-course as you imagine.

One of the best things I discovered after I had been derailed myself is that the time and skills I accumulated during the derailment helped me develop my gifts and share them with the world.

So many people are on the right track, but their beliefs don't allow them to have the awareness to recognize it.

Please don't look back and mope over the perceived loss of time. You really didn't lose any. That's because you're meant to be precisely where you are today. You're here right now, and you were meant to be here, reading this book and thinking about your talents.

Think back on your earliest memory about what you wanted to be when you grew up. Did you want to be a teacher, a pilot, a scientist, or something else? What do you remember? This doesn't mean you need to dispose of your law degree or whatever profession you have and become a hairdresser because you like working with hair and makeup. All it means is that when you were a child, you were more in tune with your natural talents.

Please know that your talents can be used inside or outside your job. For example, if you wanted to be a chef but ended up as a police officer, begin to cook. You don't need to open a restaurant to share your talents. Instead, you can volunteer at a soup kitchen, your church, or other organizations that feed the hungry. You can start baking and selling at church, farmers' markets, and other street fairs. If you want to be a writer, begin writing today. You don't even need to buy a computer. The internet is full of people looking for writers/contributors, or you can share your work on social media and personal blogs. The point is that you can begin today without quitting what you have been doing.

When you align yourself with your talents, doors will open. Of course, you can still desire to be discovered and leave your current job, but my experience has taught me that you need to stop hating your job first before the next level comes. The "hate my job" energy doesn't mix with the "love my job" energy you seek. If you continue to hate, you will continue to produce more of what you hate; and if, through the strong willpower, you get the next job, you will likely attract a similar type of experience instead of the "dream job you love." So, in a short period of time, you will hate your new job.

The key point is, please share your gifts and begin using them immediately. You have an eternity to develop and share them with the world, but why wait that long? Great chefs weren't amazing when they started.

Talents are like a seed. They need fertile soil, water, and sun to grow. How are you caring for your talents? Do you embrace them, or do you hide them in the basement of your life? Do you take time to practice, or do you resent your past choices? If you use your energy to fault the past, you're too far apart from the energy you need to share your gifts.

When I was fifteen years old, I taught guitar lessons to earn money that often helped buy food for my family. Most of my students were children and other teenagers, except for one. Lucia was the mother of a close friend. I called her Dona Lucia, which is the way we refer respectfully to mature women.

Dona Lucia was in her mid-fifties at the time when she also took up painting and sculpturing. She'd wanted to be an artist, but marriage, children, and her family's beliefs about artists had deterred her. Despite her children's mockery and her ex-husband's criticism of how Dona Lucia spent her time, she kept going and learned to paint, sculpt, and play guitar. Dona Lucia might not have sold any art pieces or played in any concerts, but she developed her talents before they died inside her. That is self-generosity.

You don't need to share your talents with the entire world—only your world—even if your audience is just you and your younger self. Make yourself proud. You and your younger self have been waiting for so long.

Chapter 9
The Power of Healing

"You have the power to heal your life,
and you need to know that."

— LOUISE L. HAY

The ninth Power of Women is the Power of Healing. This power is connected with the non-dominant hand. There is a small heart chakra in our hand, and when it's activated by our intention and connected with the heart's energy, we experience the Power of Healing. Like the Power of Generosity, there is a minor heart chakra located in the center of the palm of our hands, and it is energized by the colors green, pink, and white.

In the Gospel of Luke, Jesus sent his disciples to go into town, heal the sick, and say to them, "The kingdom of God is at hand for you." (Luke 10:9) In this passage, Jesus teaches us that we all have the ability to heal others and ourselves. In ancient history, the works of Confucius, Mencius, and Lao Tzu shared the wisdom of the healing arts through QI, the energy force in everyone.

The Power of Healing may be a bit more challenging for some of you to believe. Let's take it from the beginning and see how far we can take this power to heart. When you have a paper cut, the cut heals itself within a few days without doing much except washing it. When you have a cold and don't take anything for it, the cold goes away in a few days. How do you explain that the body heals these two different conditions on its own? How does the body know when to close a cut and when to eliminate the cold virus? We must agree that there is an intelligence inside everyone that knows how to keep us alive.

According to Chinese medicine, this energy is QI, pronounced "chi," which is in everything. It produces vitality. When this flow of liveliness is blocked, the body falls ill.

When people meditate, practice Tai Chi, yoga, QIgong, and other Eastern practices, they can feel the QI energy in their bodies. The soft-touch of a mother's hand on an aching child is another use of the healing energy force available to us. The mother's touch alone has the power to soothe the pain, stop the tears, and even help the child sleep. The mother's pure intention to take the pain away from her child is strong enough to heal, and the child's body recognizes it. However, the mother doesn't cure the child; she only facilitates the child to heal herself.

Every woman has the same potential for healing powers and the ability to create the space for others to heal. So many women are called to be healers, such as doctors, nurses, acupuncturists, chiropractors, and reiki practitioners. Others don't need to have a formal call; they become healers for themselves and their families in their communities.

I've met a fair number of healers in my life. Not all of them started their path as such. Many had, and some still have other careers. Not only do they use their hands, but also their voice, energy, water, guides, angels, and tarot cards to help others heal physical diseases and mental and spiritual uneasiness.

Because all women have the capacity to heal but not all are called to be healers, we must accept this gift with an open heart. If you've been hearing nudges from the universe about healing, you aren't alone. All women are being summoned to use their powers to heal their homes, communities, and countries. Some are being called directly to use their gifts to be natural healers and others to heal the energy of the planet. In addition, women are being called to uplift the energy of their work environments, social media communities, and religious organizations.

The most recent world events we experienced in 2016 and are still happening now in 2021 as I write this book are an indication of the instability of humankind's energy. Earth is perfect and has the ability to heal itself, as it's one of God's fabulous ideas. Unfortunately, people have been so out of alignment with their thoughts, emotions, and actions that the planet has become unbalanced. Violence, discrimination, disease, and hate have been in the air. Lives have been lost to create wake-up calls.

Many women have changed the world, some of whom haven't been recognized until recently. Rosa Parks, Emmeline Pankhurst, Rosalind Franklin, Margaret Thatcher, Sojourner Truth, Hellen Keller, Oprah Winfrey, Malala Yousafzai, and thousands of others stuck their neck out for change. Although George Floyd wasn't a woman, his voice was needed to create a more equitable world. Something must be done.

Women have taken a backseat for too many years. Our ancestors might have found the time of obscurity necessary for women to catch their breath, fuel the small fires in different corners of the world, and birth more warriors to question the status quo. Now, it's time for women with our Power of Healing to lead us toward equality.

Equitable equality is the state in which women are recognized for their diversity of thought, heard, and treated fairly, not for being women, but for being human beings who happen to think and behave differently than men.

Women could continue to impersonate men to gain a seat at the table, or we could just walk in and take two chairs, one for ourselves and another to save for the next woman to arrive. We need to save millions of seats for our sisters, mothers, and daughters. That's how we'll heal humanity.

What Are Women Called to Heal?

Women are called to heal themselves first and then the planet's consciousness by rebuilding the acceptance of our emotions, each other, and our ambitions. Men and women must work together to reconstruct the energy of community, equality, participation, and creativity, just to name a few. This job didn't fall on our plates; we signed up for it.

As we evolve, we're called to create the space for healing. This will happen in open conversations, forgiveness sessions, the truth of intentions, and most of all, the acceptance of our differences. We don't have to be the same to work together. There is an inequality of rights, resources distribution, advancement opportunities, and access to education worldwide.

It's true that sometimes when an opportunity for betterment is given to many unprivileged people, some will refuse it or take it but not use it. They don't realize that holding on just a bit longer can yield great rewards. Their beginnings taught them to give up rather than linger in hope, which is how they learned to avoid disappointment. But what they might do or not do isn't our concern. It's still our responsibility to heal and build a better world. Unfortunately, healing sometimes takes generations before fundamental changes can take place.

I believe that women, through their circles, can actively participate in the world's affairs and speak out against the decisions that don't serve humanity. For that to happen, we will need more women to step up and take on roles that have usually been reserved for men by men. We need to place our best runners at the front of the race. But, again, this isn't a race of men versus women. This is about a more equitable distribution of decisions that have lacked female input, which is consistently known for inclusion, cooperation, and compassion.

Some may argue that we have strong women already sitting at the table who don't meet my description of women or what some may call stereotypes. First, there isn't such a thing as a stereotype of women. We are all individuals. The common traits found in women, such as cooperation, sense of community, compassion, and inspired creativity, are available to all. Still, many have chosen to not use some of these strengths because of their upbringing and the environment they find themselves in. Whoever they decide to become in order to be taken seriously can't be measured against their female talents. The masculine power exercised throughout history has suppressed women's ability to be themselves. They were excluded because they happened to have a different perspective along with a vagina. The few women who were raised to the occasion were mentored by men and quickly learned to mimic the behavior of their role models in order to reach the top.

Not too long ago, one of the women who worked on my team was passed over for a promotion because she got engaged. Our boss believed that her mind would be on the wedding rather than the business. Another time, a high-performing manager didn't get promoted because she attributed her success to her personality during her interview. She used the word "bubbly," and the big boss vetoed her promotion as a result. Another consistent, long-term, high-performer went through a rough spot, and the boss shared with me that she wasn't performing as well as she did in the past because she got a new boyfriend, even though she met all the goals.

A man wouldn't be passed over for promotion for dating, getting engaged, or being extra friendly. These may seem like minor incidents, but they happen daily behind closed doors. If a woman isn't in the room to witness the discussion and at least attempt to change the outcome, these injustices will undoubtedly continue to happen.

Forgiveness Is a Space for Healing

You may have heard a saying, usually by men, that women have memories like elephants. This is because women tend to vividly remember what happened twenty, thirty, and forty years ago, often changing their mood when they recall it as if it just happened a few minutes ago.

Women never forget. This's because we recall events with our emotions. Whatever emotion we felt when an event happened caused an imprint in our memory, so we're able to remember it for as long as we want. Unfortunately, these deep emotions create a wound, which tends to be hard to let go of because they often become resentment. (Of course, this isn't true of all women, and it's also true of some men.)

Science has even discovered that we carry the DNA of our ancestors and that our hormones are programmed to react as if we were still living in caves. Our parasympathetic nervous system responds to our everyday life as if we're fighting lions and bears.

This means that we not only react to what happened last week, but we react to what happened with our ancestors. Somewhere in women's DNA, there's the history of our predecessors. The experiences of women who were denied education, considered a burden to their families, couldn't own property, didn't have the right to voice their opinion, weren't allowed to run a business, keep money, or work after marriage are inside of you. These and other injustices are all in our genetic memory. In our DNA, there is a history of the fear of advancement, speaking out, taking action, owning, practicing unpopular religion, and every other prohibition women were exposed to. It also means that we may take a safer road these days because of these traumas we carry in our bodies.

It's no wonder that we have this trauma. When I read *The History of Ideas on Woman* by Rosemary Agonito, I was horrified, livid, and even cried. I couldn't believe the theories about women over the centuries. I started to unleash my anger about the Book of Genesis, Plato, Bacon, and other idiots who fed us these ideas that women were "less than." Anytime I saw misogyny, it triggered frustration. I learned that those ideas still live on in some people, and naively, they didn't see any harm in those observations.

Plato said that women were only needed to produce heirs for men. Unfortunately, some still believe this today, and Plato is still considered to be a great philosopher. Scottish philosopher David Hume believed that women were more prone to infidelity than men. Was he on drugs? Many men still think this way today, but the data shows otherwise. I must confess that for a moment, I wanted to burn their books, remove them from all libraries in the world and curse their offsprings. Okay, it lasted a good week. But those and other imbeciles are the reason I am fueled to promote change today.

As a result of my research, I have realized that part of the healing for humanity must come through the forgiveness of the past. If you did the practice of letting go in the previous chapter, you're ready to move to the next step, which is healing through forgiveness. When we begin to let go of physical clutter, emotional clutter also loosens up, opening an opportunity to forgive everyone who has done us harm, intentionally or unintentionally.

We can use our Power of Healing to forgive anyone, even those old men from the past who added to the centuries of discrimination against women. That's a healing piece for us.

Forgiveness isn't easy, of course. How can we give others a part of ourselves when they hurt us? How can we feel compassion for those who invaded our sacred space? How can we forgive when the wound is nailed down with resentment and corroded with plans of revenge?

At first, attempts to forgive may feel like another stab in the heart. We think that people don't deserve forgiveness. But every time we rage, we sink. Then, one day, we're stuck at the bottom of the sea without the strength to swim up and out of the cage we've built with our rage. So now, tell me, who is punishing whom?

Forgiveness is a healing practice for women, and healing is an act of self-generosity. We must let go of the past to stop perpetuating the wound. Giving it more time only makes it raw and painful. It's time to heal.

You will have the opportunity to heal and forgive everyone with ease when you listen to the second meditation I added to this book. The results were too powerful to leave it for a chance. When I stumbled on the work of Colette Streicher, the founder of the MAP System, I was amazed by the results her methods achieved. The gentle approach to healing by rewiring the brain is fast and produces long-lasting results. I use her techniques on the Nine Powers of Women Quantum Activation Program - Healing

Through the Chakras #9 Power of Healing when you purchase the book. You can buy the other eight recordings if you like.

Body, Mind, and Wisdom School

Here are four additional suggestions for you to improve your Power of Healing:

One: Own Your Healing

The healing process must start with us, the women who are called to do something about it. We begin to heal by examining our thoughts that may not be our own. Unconscious bias against women may live in your psyche. You may have heard from your parents and grand-parents that women are inferior, deficient in math, best left in the home, etc. You may have unconscious beliefs that only pretty women get promoted, that you have to be skinny or use your sexuality to advance in business, or that women are too emotional to be effective.

Pick up your journal or the book companion. Write a list of all the degrading misrepresentations of women you've heard in the past.

Then, listen to the Nine Powers of Women Quantum Activation Program - Healing Through the Chakras #9 Power of Healing. Please download it from the http://www.ana-barreto.com/ninepowers

Next, cross out each of the statements you wrote and begin to erase them from your subconscious. Replace them with these statements that have been calibrated at a higher frequency by scientist David Hawkins, who measured the power of emotions, words, and events:

— Women are incredible human beings.
— Women are strong.
— Women are free to do everything they wish.
— Women are as important and smart as men.
— Women have infinite potential.
— Women can do anything their hearts desire.

After you finish listening to the Nine Powers of Women Quantum Activation Program - Healing Through the Chakras #9 Power of Healing, write down the current resistance level if you still have any.

Two: Be True to Your Calling

If you want to be the CEO, you must muster the courage and follow-through. You must honor your level of ambition regardless of what people expect of you. Don't think of the work involved, only of the outcome.

Three: Be a Healer

You are a healer. Being a healer isn't only the calling of those in the medical field. You must help, mentor, support, and counsel other women who aspire to be more. The more women we have at the table, the easier it will be to influence the outcome of inclusion, community, and compassion. We must create a space where women can be themselves and have their contributions heard and appreciated. Share this book and Meditations with them.

The more we talk about it and involve everyone in the conversation, the easier it will be for women to share their true talents with the world.

Four: Forgive Everyone

I don't remember who said, "I never forgive because I don't have anything to forgive." That's a true acceptance of others. It's a great way to go about life in our interactions with people different from us. Forgiveness isn't for them; it's for you.

As a healer, your well-being starts with the freedom to feel all of your emotions and then forgive everyone from your past. So write a list of the people you need to forgive. Then, open your heart to begin to forgive them. You could write each person a letter, but don't mail it. You can also have a conversation with their spirit and say what you need to say. This action alone will open the QI energy in your body and bring more vitality and happiness into your being. Remember that you're doing this for your own healing, not theirs. Healing of the world starts with yourself.

Chapter 10
Where Do We Go from Here?

*"Do you not see that all your misery comes from the
strange belief that you are powerless?"*

— A COURSE IN MIRACLES

My dear woman, we come to the last chapter of the book. Thank you for taking this journey with me. I am glad you've opened your spirit up to this new understanding of the truth. I know you have begun to feel and use your powers little by little to improve your life. I invite you to be fully convinced that the world needs you, just the way you are.

You are equipped with enough inspiration to continue blossoming. You have now entered the sacred garden, and you are one of the billions of flowers sharing and expanding the essence of the Divine Feminine. Being a woman is like being marvelous gifts humanity unwraps daily to celebrate life. "Happy Life to Me!" exudes from you.

Being a woman is also like a breath of fresh air for mankind. So, take those deep breaths and exercise your powers freely without apologies. You are being a *real* woman. Be the moon in the desert admired by the hopeless or the lighthouse in a storm for the lost boats at sea. You are already a pearl. You are ready to own your strengths and improve the quality of life for yourself and everyone around you. It's time to unmask your untarnished identity, the Divine Feminine, and let the world know that you have arrived.

Use your powers for good and to balance the energy in the world for everyone. If you are a bit afraid of your inherited gifts, know that it's natural, but that hesitation is just a sign that you are walking on your tiptoes. In time, you will have full footing. I have a suspicion that you already know which of your powers are strong and ready to be put to good use and which powers need more time to nurture and develop. Trust that knowing.

Which power do you like best? Which power intrigues you? And which Power are you hesitant to pursue? Get in bed with them. Sleep in their comfort and feel them in your core. You can't afford to allow your gifts to be dormant again. I'll tell you a little secret: the powers you fear the most are the powers you need to exercise the most. Trust in yourself. Your soul will support you and harvest your strength to get you going. You are not alone. You were never alone. There is an army behind your decisions; just call on the Divine Feminine, and we will answer.

Each power will build on another. Soon, you will have a good hold on all of your powers, and you'll see the improvements in your life and the world around you.

When women are nurtured, they share kindness in the world.
When women are creative, they solve problems with ease and peace.
When women are confident, they live up to their potential.
When women are compassionate, they love freely.
When women are authentic, they live truly happy lives.
When women are intuitive, they feel the truth.
When women are beautiful, they see beauty in everything.
When women are generous, they are open to giving and receiving.
When women are healers, they heal themselves and the planet.

I will leave you with a meditation to help you activate your powers. Also, there are The Further Resources, which lists issues associated with each power and a list of affirmations to help you develop and grow your strengths.

When more women exercise their right to be willing, active contributors in the decisions for humanity—such as laws, business, medicine, science, education, government, mathematics, philosophy, arts, architecture, engineering, religion, and any decision that affects people—the energy of the world becomes more balanced. That's the purpose of the Divine Feminine.

Women are the heart of humanity. We just need to beat purposefully, and we will experience the divine life force in all areas of our lives.

There is no wrong way to go from here. For the next step, you could cultivate one of the Nine Powers or start with the one you are most afraid of. Perhaps you could practice one power a week, or for one month. Some of you will be called to reread the whole book, and others will be enchanted with one Power and embark on the journey of mastery. You see, you are being guided to extend your Divine Feminine, and there is no wrong way.

The Calling

Within the words of this book, you have been called to:

Become your own mother.
Create your life with intention.
Strengthen your confidence.
Feel self-compassion.
Release your authentic self.
Trust your intuition.
See the beauty in yourself.
Be generous to receive.
Heal yourself.

How will you answer it? How will you respond to the calling of the Women of the Ancient?

Your life *is* the answer.

How you choose to live is the way to inherit the divine breath of the feminine. Can you see the infinite potential at your disposal?

Please surrender to the freedom this calling brings. This summoning only requires you to unfold your essence and flow like the wind – freely. Come and share with the world the unique gifts bestowed on you on the day you were born. Your powers will support the woman your soul has dreamed of.

Let there be unobstructed life. Let there be a woman. Let there be a story so beautiful that your ancestors will rejoice and your offspring will sing about. Let there be the amazing and blessed *you*.

NEW BEGINING

The Nine Powers
of Women Meditation

Welcome to the Nine Powers of Women Meditation. You can download this and other meditations at http://www.ana-barreto.com/meditations.

This meditation can be done any time of the day, but it's always best to do it in the morning.

The Nine Powers of Women Meditation will improve the nine energy centers of the body and awaken the Divine Feminine within.

This is a healing meditation. Through your breathing, you will increase the flow of the Qi in your body, restore your natural powers, heal your body and your life.

Once you memorize the meditation, you can do this practice to heal all of your chakras or just the blocked ones needing more energy. You can also use this practice to heal any area of the body where you feel discomfort and disease. Please note that this meditation is not a substitute for medical treatment. However, you can use it in conjunction with your doctor's advice.

1. Find a comfortable place and time when you won't be interrupted for at least fifteen to twenty minutes. Sit comfortably in a chair, on a bed, or on a pillow.
2. Rest your hands on your lap or chair and uncross your legs.
3. Take three long and slow breaths. Breathe in and out through your nose.
4. Breathe in and breathe out.

5. Breathe in and breathe out.
6. Close your eyes to minimize distractions. Every noise you hear will take you deeper and deeper into the meditation. This is a healing practice.
7. Place your attention on your heart center and continue to breathe.
8. Breathe in and breathe out.
9. Breathe in and breathe out.
10. Stay in your heart.
11. Breathe in and breathe out.
12. Breathe in and breathe out.
13. Continue to breathe slowly and take deep breaths.
14. Imagine the breath coming in and out through your heart.
15. Feel compassion and gratitude as you breathe in and out.
16. Breathe in and breathe out with a sense of inner happiness. You can feel the healing energy from your heart.
17. Breathe in and breathe out.
18. Allow the breath to exit through the lower part of your heart center very slowly.
19. Breathe in and imagine the breath going out through the second chakra at your belly button.
20. Keep feeling a sense of gratitude and inner happiness.
21. Imagine the breath coming in through the skin of your whole body.
22. As you exhale, see it exiting through the lower part of your heart center.
23. Breathe in through your whole body.
24. Breathe out through your belly button.
25. Breathe in through your entire body.
26. Breathe out through your belly button.
27. Keep feeling a sense of happiness and know that you are healing your body.
28. Breathe in through your entire body.
29. Breathe out through the root chakra located in the base of your spine. Do this three times to awaken the Power of Nurturing.

30. Breathe in through your entire body.
31. Breathe out through your root chakra.
32. Breathe in through your whole body.
33. Breathe out through your root chakra.
34. Let's awaken the Power of Creativity. Breathe in through your entire body.
35. Breathe out through your belly button, the sacral chakra.
36. Breathe in through your whole body.
37. Breathe out through your belly button.
38. Breathe in through your entire body.
39. Breathe out through your belly button.
40. Let's awaken the Power of Confidence. See the breath entering your body through every inch of your skin.
41. Breathe out through the solar plexus located above your belly below your breasts.
42. Breathe in through your entire body.
43. Breathe out through your solar plexus.
44. Breathe in through your whole body.
45. Breathe out through your solar plexus.
46. Let's awaken the Power of Compassion. Breathe in through your entire body.
47. Breathe out through your heart center, located in the middle of your chest.
48. Breathe in through your entire body.
49. Breathe out through your heart center.
50. Breathe in through your whole body.
51. Breathe out through your heart center.
52. Let's awaken the Power of Authenticity. Breathe in through your entire body.
53. Breathe out through your throat chakra located in the middle of your throat.
54. Breathe in through your entire body.
55. Breathe out through your throat center.
56. Breathe in through your whole body.
57. Breathe out through your throat center.

58. Let's awaken the Power of Intuition. Breathe in through your entire body.
59. Breathe out through your third eye chakra, located between your eyebrows.
60. Breathe in through your whole body.
61. Breathe out through your third eye.
62. Breathe in through your entire body.
63. Breathe out through your third eye.
64. Let's awaken the Power of Beauty through the crown chakra located at the top of your head.
65. Breathe in through your whole body.
66. Breathe out through your crown chakra.
67. Breathe in through your entire body.
68. Breathe out through your crown chakra.
69. Breathe in through your whole body.
70. Breathe out through your crown chakra.
71. Let's awaken the Power of Generosity through the small heart chakra located on the palm of your dominant hand.
72. Breathe in through your entire body.
73. Breathe out through the palm of your dominant hand.
74. Breathe in through your entire body.
75. Breathe out through the palm of your dominant hand.
76. Breathe in through your entire body.
77. Breathe out through the palm of your dominant hand.
78. Let's awaken the Power of Healing through the small heart chakra located on the palm of your non-dominant hand.
79. Breathe in through your entire body.
80. Breathe out through the palm of your non-dominant hand.
81. Breathe in through your whole body.
82. Breathe out through the palm of your non-dominant hand.
83. Breathe in through your entire body.
84. Breathe out through the palm of your non-dominant hand.
85. Breathe in through your whole body.
86. Breathe out through your belly button.
87. Breathe in through your whole body.

88. Breathe out through any area of your body where you feel discomfort, acute pain, or even chronic pain.
89. Find an area in your body that needs healing and use your QI breath to heal it.
90. When you're ready, open your eyes, rub your palms together, and return to your day.
91. Thank you for meditating with me.

Further Resources

Here is a guide to help you identify the issues associated with the powers that need development. Also, there are daily affirmations to help you strengthen them. Read them out loud, repeat them throughout the day, post them on your mirror, bedroom, wallet, or in your office to support your work:

POWER OF NURTURING

ISSUES: Lack of self-care (eat, sleep, rest, downtime, grooming), issues with mother or daughter, burnout, stress, overworked, problems with money and jobs, anxiety, urinary infections, sexual diseases, and pregnancy.

AFFIRMATION: *"I am safe. I am supported. I am loved."*

POWER OF CREATIVITY

ISSUES: Overeating, bulimia, over-drinking, using drugs, high or no libido, sex addiction, depression, over/underweight, diabetes, and kidney issues.

AFFIRMATION: *"I accept my life purpose and manifest a beautiful life."*

POWER OF CONFIDENCE

ISSUES: Low confidence, low energy, procrastination, low self-esteem, lack of self-trust, controlling, being controlled, self-sabotage, incomplete tasks, panic attacks, freezing under pressure, anger, stomach issues.

AFFIRMATION: *"I am willing to release all outcomes."*

POWER OF COMPASSION

ISSUES: Resentment, problems in past and current relationships, codependency, holding grudges, not forgiving, lack of self-love, always being the good girl, grief, high/low blood pressure, heart disease.

AFFIRMATION: *"I forgive myself and everyone, and I know that we are all learning."*

POWER OF AUTHENTICITY

ISSUES: Lies, don't speak up, don't make decisions, insecurity, pretending, showing off, comparing self with others, jealousy, sore throat, anger, aggressiveness.

AFFIRMATION: *"I release all my fears and reservations, and I enjoy being me."*

POWER OF INTUITION

ISSUES: Indecision, lack of clarity, confusion, chaos, stubbornness, busyness, vertigo, lack of self-trust, using tarot cards, psychics, angel cards, etc. too often, vision issues.

AFFIRMATION: *"It's safe for me to see the truth."*

POWER OF BEAUTY

ISSUES: No spiritual connection or practice, lack of trust in a higher power, pessimism, disconnection with nature, lack of purpose, unhappiness, headaches, migraines, memory loss.

> AFFIRMATION: *"I trust the in and out flow of wisdom and my inner guidance."*

POWER OF GENEROSITY

ISSUES: Overwhelmed, overworked, over-giving, holding on to things, physical and mental clutter, not asking for or receiving help, not forgiving, itchy hands.

> AFFIRMATION: *"I honor the flow of giving and receiving."*

POWER OF HEALING

ISSUES: No life purpose, constantly sick, recurring diseases, bitterness, hate working, continually complaining, disconnection with love/heart, lack of sleep.

> AFFIRMATION: *"I heal my body and my life with loving thoughts."*

Bibliography

The Bible, Catholic Bible

Parks, Anton. *Searching for the Garden of Eden* (Gaia, 2017 October)

Ovchinnikov IV, Götherström A, Romanova GP, Kharitonov VM, Lidén K, Goodwin W. *Molecular analysis of Neanderthal DNA from the northern Caucasus* (Nature, 2000 Mar 30)

Wauter, Ambika, The *Book of Chakras: Discover the Hidden Forces Within You.* (2002 Quarto Inc.)

Hissong, Samantha, Finally, *Research Suggests Female Artists Are More Creative Than Men.* (Rolling Stone March 6, 2020)

Adams, Kate, *Even Women Think Men Are More Creative.* (Harvard Business Review December 2015)

Biography.com Editors, Mary Shelley Biography. (A&E Television Networks The Biography.com May 6, 2021)

Gimbutas, Marija. T*he Goddesses and Gods of Old Europe: Myths and Cult Images, New and Updated Edition* (1982, University of California Press)

Darwin, Charles. *On the Origin of Species by Means of Natural Selection, or The Preservation of Favoured Races in the Struggle for Life* (2010, FQ Books)

Desai, Rajvi. *We've Completely Misunderstood 'Survival of the Fittest,' Evolutionary Biologists Say* (The Swaddle.com Oct 6, 2020)

Mirgain, Shilagh. *The Healing Power of Music.* (UWHealth.org May 22, 2019)

Agonito, Rosemary. *The History of Ideas on Woman: A Source Book.* (Capricorn Books, 1977)

Holden, Robert, *Loveability: Knowing How to Love and Be Loved* (Hay House 2013)

Maslow, A H. A Theory of Human Motivation (2017 BN Publishing)

Pinkola Estes, Clarissa, *Women Who Run with the Wolves: Myths and Stories of the Wild Woman Archetype* (Ballantine Books, 1996)

Cohen, Julie, West, Betsey, *My Name is Pauli Murray* (Amazon Documentary 2021)

Hawkins, David R, *Letting Go: The Pathway to Surrender* (Hay House 2012)

Wilson Jr., Vincent McClung, Gale, *The book of Distinguished American Women* (2003, American History Research Association Publication)

SantoPietro, Nancy, *Feng Shui: Harmony by Design* (Berkley Publishing Group 1996)

Diemer, Deedre, ABC's of Chakra Therapy: A Workbook (Weiser Books 1998)

About the Author

Ana Barreto is a Brazilian-American teacher, author, and coach living in upstate New York. At eighteen years of age, she left her parents' traditional patriarchal home in Rio de Janeiro, Brazil, and broke the established female roles of her upbringing. Two years later, she moved to New York and began her college education.

While attending Marymount College, at that time a women-only institution, Ana began to learn about women's rights and empowerment. Her passion for women's development and growth led her to study psychology, women in history, business, and leadership, meditation, spirituality, and Eastern philosophies. She holds Bachelor's and Master's degrees in Business Administration.

In 2016, Ana published her first book, *Women, Rice and Beans – Nine Wisdoms I Learned from My Mother When I Really Paid Attention*. She hopes to inspire women who are overwhelmed in their lives to find daily wisdom and break the old patterns of thinking, believing, and being that don't honor their spirit.

In her second book, *Self-Trust – A Healing Practice for Women Who Work Too Much*, published in 2018, Ana shared sixteen healing practices to help women trust themselves and change old mindset patterns that don't serve humanity.

In *There is a Higher Power Within – 28 Meditation Prompts to Find Peace & Happiness Within*, Ana shared an easy meditation practice for busy people, including daily reflection and gratitude prompts.

Ana's purpose is to help people improve the quality of their lives. Her mission is to inspire, guide, and coach women through her books, classes, meditations, and inspirational material, helping them find their inner compass and live great lives.

When Ana isn't working or writing books, she enjoys cooking, traveling, hiking, biking, kayaking, and spending time with her partner, Jim, her daughters Erica and Isabel, her stepdaughters Cindy, Janet, and Christine, and her friends.

Printed in Great Britain
by Amazon

87764065R00129